Driving Data Quality with Data Contracts

A comprehensive guide to building reliable, trusted, and effective data platforms

Andrew Jones

BIRMINGHAM—MUMBAI

Driving Data Quality with Data Contracts

Group Product Manager: Reshma Raman

Publishing Product Manager: Apeksha Shetty

Senior Editor: Nathanya Dias

Technical Editor: Kavyashree K S

Copy Editor: Safis Editing

Project Coordinator: Farheen Fathima

Proofreader: Safis Editing

Indexer: Manju Arasan

Production Designer: Prashant Ghare

Marketing Coordinator: Nivedita Singh

First published: July 2023

Production reference: 1300623

Published by Packt Publishing Ltd.

Livery Place

35 Livery Street

Birmingham

B3 2PB, UK.

ISBN 978-1-83763-500-9

www.packtpub.com

To my wife, Debs, for all your love and support, and my children, Alex and Rosie – your laughter is my favorite sound.

– Andrew Jones

Foreword

An ounce of prevention is worth a pound of cure. This nugget of wisdom holds true in both the worlds of health and data. Unfortunately, trust in data is easily lost and hard to regain. Data contracts have taken our community by storm as a socio-technical solution to achieve and maintain high levels of trust.

My first exposure to data contracts was through Andrew's presentation at a data quality meetup in London, hosted at the headquarters of a popular grocery chain. He and I both spoke at the meetup, although I was happy to be overshadowed. The room was rapt as he painted a picture of the whys, whats, and hows of data contracts at GoCardless. Most of us were only familiar with data contracts as a buzzword, but here Andrew is showing us the actual YAML specifications.

I remember that the Q&A portion was overflowing with questions for Andrew and we had to cut the section short. Thankfully, this book answers all of the questions I had.

Like his talk, this book is a bridge between theory and practice. *Chapter 1, A Brief History of Data Platforms*, paired with *Chapter 7, Contract-Driven Data Architecture*, provide a strong conceptual foundation for data contracts. The final two chapters, *Chapter 9, Implementing Data Contracts in Your Organization*, and *Chapter 10, Data Contracts in Practice*, provide powerful tools to think about the practice of data contracts.

Along the way, as a reader, I am grateful for how the book progressively introduces complexity, interweaves real examples between explanations, and leaves me with opportunities to learn further. Whether you're a data practitioner who is tired of being blamed for data quality issues or a business stakeholder who wants to promote data trust, this book is the gold standard for learning about data contracts.

Kevin Hu, PhD

Co-founder and CEO at Metaplane

Contributors

About the author

Andrew Jones is a principal engineer at GoCardless, one of Europe's leading Fintech's. He has over 15 years experience in the industry, with the first half primarily as a software engineer, before he moved into the data infrastructure and data engineering space. Joining GoCardless as its first data engineer, he led his team to build their data platform from scratch. After initially following a typical data architecture and getting frustrated with facing the same old challenges he'd faced for years, he started thinking there must be a better way, which led to him coining and defining the ideas around *data contracts*. Andrew is a regular speaker and writer, and he is passionate about helping organizations get maximum value from data.

Thanks to everyone at GoCardless who supported me in taking data contracts from a one-pager to successful implementation, and then an industry topic worthy of an entire book! Also, a big thank you to everyone in the data community who has been so generous with their time and helped develop the ideas that became data contracts.

About the reviewers

John Thomas, a data analytics architect and dedicated book reviewer, combines his passion for data and technology in his work. He has successfully designed and implemented data warehouses, lakes, and meshes for organizations worldwide. With expertise in data integration, ETL processes, governance, and streaming, John's eloquent book reviews resonate with both tech enthusiasts and book lovers. His reviews offer insights into the evolving technological landscape shaping the publishing industry.

Animesh Kumar is the CTO and co-founder @Modern, and the co-creator of the **Data Developer Platform** (DDP) infrastructure specification. With over 20 years in the data engineering space, Animesh has donned multiple hats, including those of architect, VP engineer, CTO, CPO, and founder, across a wide range of technology firms. He has architected engineering solutions for several A-players, including the likes of the NFL, Gap, Verizon, Rediff, Reliance, SGWS, Gensler, and TOI. He is presently dedicated to building DataOS as a direct implementation of the DDP infrastructure specification.

Table of Contents

Part 2: Driving Data Culture Change with Data Contracts

3

4

5

Part 3: Designing and Implementing a Data Architecture Based on Data Contracts

6

7

8

9

Implementing Data Contracts in Your Organization   141

10

Data Contracts in Practice   159

Preface

Hello, and welcome to *Driving Data Quality with Data Contracts*! I'm excited to share with you everything I've learned about how data contracts solve some of the age-old problems we have in our data architectures, where, despite huge investments, we rarely have easy access to good-quality data that can be used to drive real business value.

This book and the ideas behind it have been three years in the making. It was in August 2020 when I started thinking about the problems I wanted to solve at GoCardless and started calling my solution *data contracts*, before writing about them publicly for the first time in April 2021, and describing our implementation in December 2021. Since then, they've really taken off, with countless articles, presentations, and podcasts around the subject.

Over that time, I've been lucky enough to have the opportunity to speak to many people in the data community, at organizations large and small, and through those discussions I have found that while, for each of us, our data is unique, our problems are not! In fact, they're universal.

Data contracts solve these problems in two ways. The first is the implementation of a contract-backed architecture, which empowers the creation, management, and use of quality data through self-served, autonomous tooling.

The second is by changing our data culture to one where data is generated explicitly to meet use cases, where data generators and data consumers work closely together as partners, and where we focus on the quality of our data, not the quantity.

These go together, and both are required if we're going to achieve our goal of driving a truly data-driven organization that creates real business value through the effective use of quality data.

Who this book is for

If you're an experienced data engineer, data leader, architect, or practitioner thinking about your data architecture and how to design one that enables your organization to get the most value from your data, this book is for you. You should be aware of the challenges your organization has with its data and open to new approaches to solving them.

What this book covers

Chapter 1, A Brief History of Data Platforms, looks at how, despite advances in technology, by not advancing architecture, we haven't managed to move away from the same old problems of data lacking quality and failing to deliver business value.

Chapter 2, Introducing Data Contracts, introduces data contracts as the solution to those problems. We'll provide a definition and discuss the four principles that underpin data contracts. We'll also discuss how data contracts relate to data mesh.

Chapter 3, How to Get Adoption in Your Organization, starts us on the journey toward implementing and deploying data contracts, and the culture change needed for a successful adoption. We'll also discuss the idea of data products and why applying a product mindset to your data is so important.

Chapter 4, Bringing Data Consumers and Generators Closer Together, looks at why it's so important to bring these groups of people much closer together. We'll define those roles and be clear on the responsibilities and accountabilities of each.

Chapter 5, Embedding Data Governance, discusses why data governance is so important and how, by embedding it into data contracts, we can unlock a range of automations that makes it easy to manage our data.

Chapter 6, What Makes Up a Data Contract, looks at exactly what makes up a data contract, including the schema. We'll also discuss how to support the evolution of data, while still providing data consumers the stability they need to build on data with confidence.

Chapter 7, A Contract-Driven Data Architecture, shows how to use data contracts to drive our data architecture. We explain why this is a step-change in how we build data platforms, promoting the autonomous self-service of effective data tooling.

Chapter 8, A Sample Implementation, puts the concepts we have been learning into practice by building an end-to-end sample implementation of data contracts.

Chapter 9, Implementing Data Contracts in Your Organization, discusses how to get started with data contracts in your organization, building that up with the tooling and culture change required until you reach maturity.

Chapter 10, Data Contracts in Practice, looks at how we work with data contracts on a day-to-day level, including designing a data contract, monitoring and enforcement, and publishing patterns for data generators.

To get the most out of this book

For the sample implementation in *Chapter 8, A Sample Implementation*, you will need to have a basic understanding of the command line, Python, Docker, and Google Cloud.

Software/hardware covered in the book	Operating system requirements
Python 3.9.12	Windows, macOS, or Linux
Docker	Windows, macOS, or Linux
Google Cloud Platform	

If you are using the digital version of this book, we advise you to type the code yourself or access the code from the book's GitHub repository (a link is available in the next section). Doing so will help you avoid any potential errors related to the copying and pasting of code.

Much of this book is about the concept of data contracts and how we can use them to solve the key problems we have when attempting to drive business value from data. Only *Chapter 8, A Sample Implementation*, assumes this technical knowledge.

Download the example code files

You can download the example code files for this book from GitHub at https://github.com/PacktPublishing/Driving-Data-Quality-with-Data-Contracts/tree/main. If there's an update to the code, it will be updated in the GitHub repository.

We also have other code bundles from our rich catalog of books and videos available at https://github.com/PacktPublishing/. Check them out!

Conventions used

There are a number of text conventions used throughout this book.

`Code in text`: Indicates code words in text, database table names, folder names, filenames, file extensions, pathnames, dummy URLs, user input, and Twitter handles. Here is an example: "We've created a `DataContract` class to hold our data contract-related code, which you can find in `lib/data_contracts.py`."

A block of code is set as follows:

```
import pulumi
from pulumi_gcp import bigquery
default_dataset = bigquery.Dataset(
    "defaultDataset",dataset_id="pulumi_introduction",
    friendly_name="Pulumi Introduction",
    description="This is an example description",
```

When we wish to draw your attention to a particular part of a code block, the relevant lines or items are set in bold:

```
Config:
gcp:project:my-google-project-2468
```

Any command-line input or output is written as follows:

```
$ python3 -m venv venv
$ pip install -r requirements.txt
```

Bold: Indicates a new term, an important word, or words that you see on screen. For instance, words in menus or dialog boxes appear in **bold**. Here is an example: "Select **System info** from the **Administration** panel."

> **Tips or important notes**
> Appear like this.

Get in touch

Feedback from our readers is always welcome.

General feedback: If you have questions about any aspect of this book, email us at customercare@packtpub.com and mention the book title in the subject of your message.

Errata: Although we have taken every care to ensure the accuracy of our content, mistakes do happen. If you have found a mistake in this book, we would be grateful if you would report this to us. Please visit www.packtpub.com/support/errata and fill in the form.

Piracy: If you come across any illegal copies of our works in any form on the internet, we would be grateful if you would provide us with the location address or website name. Please contact us at copyright@packtpub.com with a link to the material.

If you are interested in becoming an author: If there is a topic that you have expertise in and you are interested in either writing or contributing to a book, please visit authors.packtpub.com.

Share Your Thoughts

Once you've read *Driving Data Quality with Data Contracts*, we'd love to hear your thoughts! Scan the QR code below to go straight to the Amazon review page for this book and share your feedback.

https://packt.link/r/1837635005

Your review is important to us and the tech community and will help us make sure we're delivering excellent quality content.

Download a free PDF copy of this book

Thanks for purchasing this book!

Do you like to read on the go but are unable to carry your print books everywhere? Is your eBook purchase not compatible with the device of your choice?

Don't worry, now with every Packt book you get a DRM-free PDF version of that book at no cost.

Read anywhere, any place, on any device. Search, copy, and paste code from your favorite technical books directly into your application.

The perks don't stop there, you can get exclusive access to discounts, newsletters, and great free content in your inbox daily

Follow these simple steps to get the benefits:

1. Scan the QR code or visit the link below

https://packt.link/free-ebook/978-1-83763-500-9

2. Submit your proof of purchase
3. That's it! We'll send your free PDF and other benefits to your email directly

Part 1:
Why Data Contracts?

In this part, we will look briefly at the history of data platforms and how that led us to our current state, where data is unreliable, untrustworthy, and unable to drive real business value. We'll then introduce data contracts, what they are, their guiding principles, and how they solves those problems.

This part comprises the following chapters:

1

A Brief History of Data Platforms

Before we can appreciate why we need to make a fundamental shift to a **data contracts**-backed data platform in order to improve the quality of our data, and ultimately the value we can get from that data, we need to understand the problems we are trying to solve. I've found the best way to do this is to look back at the recent generations of data architectures. By doing that, we'll see that despite the vast improvements in the tooling available to us, we've been carrying through the same limitations in the architecture. That's why we continue to struggle with the same old problems.

Despite these challenges, the importance of data continues to grow. As it is used in more and more business-critical applications, we can no longer accept data platforms that are unreliable, untrusted, and ineffective. We must find a better way.

By the end of this chapter, we'll have explored the three most recent generations of data architectures at a high level, focusing on just the source and ingestion of upstream data, and the consumption of data downstream. We will gain an understanding of their limitations and bottlenecks and why we need to make a change. We'll then be ready to learn about data contracts.

In this chapter, we're going to cover the following main topics:

- The enterprise data warehouse
- The big data platform
- The modern data stack
- The state of today's data platforms
- The ever-increasing use of data in business-critical applications

The enterprise data warehouse

We'll start by looking at the data architecture that was prevalent in the late 1990s and early 2000s, which was centered around an **enterprise data warehouse** (**EDW**). As we discuss the architecture and its limitations, you'll start to notice how many of those limitations continue to affect us today, despite over 20 years of advancement in tools and capabilities.

EDW is the collective term for a reporting and analytics solution. You'd typically engage with one or two big vendors who would provide these capabilities for you. It was expensive and only larger companies that could justify the investment.

The architecture was built around a large database in the center. This was likely an Oracle or MS SQL Server database, hosted on-premises (this was before the advent of cloud services). The **extract, transform, and load** (**ETL**) process was performed on data from source systems, or more accurately, the underlying database of those systems. That data could then be used to drive reporting and analytics.

The following diagram shows the EDW architecture:

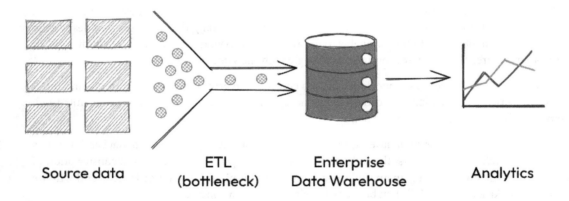

| Source data | ETL
(bottleneck) | Enterprise
Data Warehouse | Analytics |

Figure 1.1 – The EDW architecture

Because this ETL ran against the database of the source system, reliability was a problem. It created a load on the database that could negatively impact the performance of the upstream service. That, and the limitations of the technology we were using at the time, meant we could do few transforms on the data.

We also had to update the ETL process as the database schema and the data evolved over time, relying on the data generators to let us know when that happened. Otherwise, the pipeline would fail.

Those who owned databases were somewhat aware of the ETL work and the business value it drove. There were few barriers between the data generators and consumers and good communication.

However, the major limitation of this architecture was the database used for the data warehouse. It was very expensive and, as it was deployed on-premises, was of a fixed size and hard to scale. That created a limit on how much data could be stored there and made available for analytics.

It became the responsibility of the ETL developers to decide what data should be available, depending on the business needs, and to build and maintain that ETL process by getting access to the source systems and their underlying databases.

And so, this is where the bottleneck was. The ETL developers had to control what data went in, and they were the only ones who could make data available in the warehouse. Data would only be made available if it met a strong business need, and that typically meant the only data in the warehouse was data that drove the company KPIs. If you wanted some data to do some analysis and it wasn't already in there, you had to put a ticket in their backlog and hope for the best. If it did ever get prioritized, it was probably too late for what you wanted it for.

> **Note**
>
> Let's illustrate how different roles worked together with this architecture with an example.
>
> Our data generator, Vivianne, is a software engineer working on a service that writes its data to a database. She's aware that some of the data from that database is extracted by a data analyst, Bukayo, and that is used to drive top-level business KPIs.
>
> Bukayo can't do much transformation on the data, due to the limitations of the technology and the cost of infrastructure, so the reporting he produces is largely on the raw data.
>
> There are *no defined expectations* between Vivianne and Bukayo, and Bukayo relies on Vivianne telling him in advance whether there are any changes to the data or the schema.
>
> The extraction *is not reliable*. The ETL process could affect the performance of the database, and so can be switched off when there is an incident. Schema and data changes are not always known in advance. The downstream database also has limited performance and cannot be easily scaled to deal with an increase in the data or usage.
>
> Both Vivianne and Bukayo *lack autonomy*. Vivianne can't change her database schema without getting approval from Bukayo. Bukayo can only get a subset of data, with little say over the format. Furthermore, any potential users downstream of Bukayo can only access the data he has extracted, severely limiting the accessibility of the organization's data.

This won't be the last time we see a bottleneck that prevents access to, and the use of, quality data. Let's look now at the next generation of data architecture and the introduction of big data, which was made possible by the release of Apache Hadoop in 2006.

The big data platform

As the internet took off in the 1990s and the size and importance of data grew with it, the big tech companies started developing a new generation of data tooling and architectures that aimed to reduce the cost of storing and transforming vast quantities of data. In 2003, Google wrote a paper describing their Google File System, and in 2004 followed that up with another paper, titled *MapReduce: Simplified Data Processing on Large Clusters*. These ideas were then implemented at Yahoo! and open sourced as **Apache Hadoop** in 2006.

Apache Hadoop contained two core modules. The **Hadoop Distributed File System (HDFS)** gave us the ability to store almost limitless amounts of data reliably and efficiently on commodity hardware. Then the **MapReduce** engine gives us a model on which we could implement programs to process and transform this data, at scale, also on commodity hardware.

This led to the popularization of big data, which was the collective term for our reporting, ML, and analytics capabilities with HDFS and MapReduce as the foundation. These platforms used open source technology and could be on-premises or in the cloud. The reduced costs made this accessible to organizations of any size, who could either implement it themselves or use a packaged enterprise solution provided by the likes of Cloudera and MapR.

The following diagram shows the reference data platform architecture built upon Hadoop:

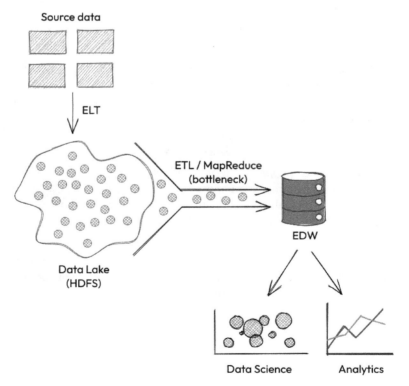

Figure 1.2 – The big data platform architecture

At the center of the architecture is the **data lake**, implemented on top of HDFS or a similar filesystem. Here, we could store an almost unlimited amount of semi-structured or unstructured data. This still needed to be put into an EDW in order to drive analytics, as data visualization tools such as Tableau needed a SQL-compatible database to connect to.

Because there were no expectations set on the structure of the data in the data lake, and no limits on the amount of data, it was very easy to write as much as you could and worry about how to use it later. This led to the concept of **extract, load, and transform** (**ELT**), as opposed to ETL, where the idea was to extract and load the data into the data lake first without any processing, then apply schemas and transforms later as part of loading to the data warehouse or reading the data in other downstream processes.

We then had much more data than ever before. With a low barrier to entry and cheap storage, data was easily added to the data lake, whether there was a consumer requirement in mind or not.

However, in practice, much of that data was never used. For a start, it was almost impossible to know what data was in there and how it was structured. It lacked any documentation, had no set expectations on its reliability and quality, and no governance over how it was managed. Then, once you did find some data you wanted to use, you needed to write MapReduce jobs using Hadoop or, later, Apache Spark. But this was very difficult to do – particularly at any scale – and only achievable by a large team of specialist data engineers. Even then, those jobs tended to be unreliable and have unpredictable performance.

This is why we started hearing people refer to it as the *data swamp*. While much of the data was likely valuable, the inaccessibility of the data lake meant it was never used. Gartner introduced the term *dark data* to describe this, where data is collected and never used, and the costs of storing and managing that data outweigh any value gained from it (`https://www.gartner.com/en/information-technology/glossary/dark-data`). In 2015, IDC estimated 90% of unstructured data could be considered dark (`https://www.kdnuggets.com/2015/11/importance-dark-data-big-data-world.html`).

Another consequence of this architecture was that it moved the end data consumers further away from the data generators. Typically, a central data engineering team was introduced to focus solely on ingesting the data into the data lake, building the tools and the connections required to do that from as many source systems as possible. They were the ones interacting with the data generators, not the ultimate consumers of the data.

So, despite the advance in tools and technologies, in practice, we still had many of the same limitations as before. Only a limited amount of data could be made available for analysis and other uses, and we had that same bottleneck controlling what that data was.

> **Note**
>
> Let's return to our example to illustrate how different roles worked together with this architecture.
>
> Our data generator, Vivianne, is a software engineer working on a service that writes its data to a database. She may or may not be aware that some of the data from that database is extracted in a raw form, and is unlikely to know exactly what the data is. Certainly, she doesn't know *why*.
>
> Ben is a data engineer who works on the ELT pipeline. He aims to extract as much of the data as possible into the data lake. He doesn't know much about the data itself, or what it will be used for. He spends a lot of time dealing with changing schemas that break his pipelines.
>
> Leah is another data engineer, specializing in writing MapReduce jobs. She takes requirements from data analysts and builds datasets to meet those requirements. She struggles to find the data she wants and needs to learn a lot about the upstream services and their data models in order to produce what she hopes is the right data. These MapReduce jobs have unpredictable performance and are difficult to debug. The jobs do not run reliably.
>
> The BI analyst, Bukayo, takes this data and creates reports to support the business. They often break due to an issue upstream. There are *no expectations* defined at any of these steps, and therefore *no guarantees on the reliability or correctness of the data* can be provided to those consuming Bukayo's data.
>
> The data generator, Vivianne, is far away from the data consumer, Bukayo, and there is no communication. Vivianne has no understanding of how the changes she makes affect key business processes.
>
> While Bukayo and his peers can usually get the data they need prioritized by Leah and Ben, those who are not BI analysts and want data for other needs *lack the autonomy* and the expertise to access it, preventing the use of data for anything other than the most critical business requirements.

The next generation of data architectures began in 2012 with the launch of Amazon Redshift on AWS and the explosion of tools and investment into what became known as the **modern data stack** (**MDS**). In the next section, we'll explore this architecture and see whether we can finally get rid of this bottleneck.

The modern data stack

Amazon Redshift was the first cloud-native data warehouse and provided a real step-change in capabilities. It had the ability to store almost limitless data at a low cost in a SQL-compatible database, and the **massively parallel processing** (**MPP**) capabilities meant you could process that data effectively and efficiently at scale.

This sounds like what we had with Hadoop, but the key differences were the SQL compatibility and the more strongly defined structure of the data. This made it much more *accessible* than the unstructured files on an HDFS cluster. It also presented an opportunity to build services on top of Redshift and later SQL-compatible warehouses such as Google BigQuery and Snowflake, which led to an explosion of tools that make up today's **modern data stack**. This includes ELT tools such as Fivetran and Stitch, data transformation tools such as dbt, and reverse ETL tools such as Hightouch.

These data warehouses evolved further to become what we now call a **data lakehouse**, which brings together the benefits of a modern data warehouse (SQL compatibility and high performance with MPP) with the benefits of a data lake (low cost, limitless storage, and support for different data types).

Into this data lakehouse went all the source data we ingested from our systems and third-party services, becoming our **operational data store** (**ODS**). From here, we could join and transform the data and make it available to our **EDW**, from where it is available for consumption. But the data warehouse was no longer a separate database – it was just a logically separate area of our data lakehouse, using the same technology. This reduced the effort and costs of the transforms and further increased the accessibility of the data.

The following diagram shows the reference architecture of the modern data stack, with the data lakehouse in the center:

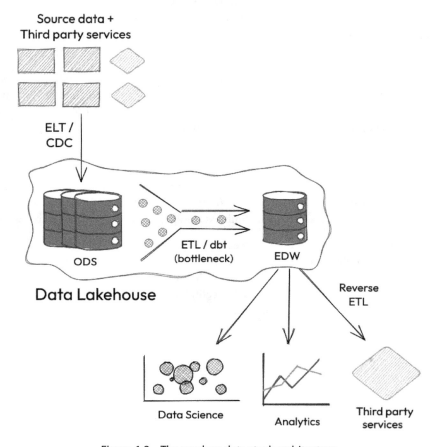

Figure 1.3 – The modern data stack architecture

This architecture gives us more options to ingest the source data, and one of those is using **change data capture** (**CDC**) tooling, for which we have open source implementations such as Debezium and commercial offerings such as Striim and Google Cloud Datastream, as well as in-depth write-ups on closed source solutions at organizations including Airbnb (https://medium.com/airbnb-engineering/capturing-data-evolution-in-a-service-oriented-architecture-72f7c643ee6f) and Netflix (https://netflixtechblog.com/dblog-a-generic-change-data-capture-framework-69351fb9099b). CDC tools connect to the transactional databases of your upstream servers and capture all the changes that happen to each of the tables (i.e., the INSERT, UPDATE, and DELETE statements run against the database). These are sent to the data lakehouse, and from there, you can recreate the database in the lakehouse with the same structure and the same data.

However, this creates a tight coupling between the internal models of the upstream service and database and the data consumers. As that service naturally evolves over time, breaking changes will be made to those models. When these happen – often without any notice – they impact the CDC service and/ or downstream data uses, leading to instability and unreliability. This makes it impossible to build on this data with any confidence.

The data is also not structured well for analytical queries and uses. It has been designed to meet the needs of the service and to be optimal for a transactional database, not a data lakehouse. It can take a lot of transformation and joining to take this data and produce something that meets the requirements of your downstream users, which is time-consuming and expensive.

There is often little or no documentation for this data, and so to make use of it you need to have in-depth knowledge of those source systems and the way they model the data, including the history of how that has evolved over time. This typically comes from asking teams who work on that service or relying on institutional knowledge from colleagues who have worked with that data before. This makes it difficult to discover new or useful datasets, or for a new consumer to get started.

The root cause of all these problems is that *this data was not built for consumption*.

Many of these same problems apply to data ingested from a third-party service through an ELT tool such as Fivetran or Stitch. This is particularly true if you're ingesting from a complex service such as Salesforce, which is highly customizable with custom objects and fields. The data is in a raw form that mimics the API of the third-party service, lacks documentation, and requires in-depth knowledge of the service to use. Like with CDC, it can still change without notice and requires a lot of transformation to produce something that meets your requirements.

One purported benefit of the modern data stack is that we now have more data available to us than ever before. However, a 2022 report from Seagate (`https://www.seagate.com/gb/en/our-story/rethink-data/`) found that 68% of the data available to organizations goes unused. We still have our dark data problem from the big data era.

The introduction of dbt and similar tools that run on a data lakehouse has made it easier than ever to process this data using just SQL – one of the most well-known and popular languages around. This should increase the accessibility of the data in the data lakehouse.

However, due to the complexity of the transforms required to make use of this data and the domain knowledge you must build up, we still often end up with a central team of data engineers to build and maintain the hundreds, thousands, or even tens of thousands of models required to produce data that is ready for consumption by other data practitioners and users.

> **Note**
>
> We'll return to our example for the final time to illustrate how different roles work together with this architecture.
>
> Our data generator, Vivianne, is a software engineer working on a service that writes its data to a database. She may or may not be aware that the data from that database is extracted in a raw form through a CDC service. Certainly, she doesn't know *why*.
>
> Ben is a data platform engineer who works on the CDC pipeline. He aims to extract as much of the data as possible into the data lakehouse. He doesn't know much about the data itself, or what it will be used for. He spends a lot of time dealing with changing schemas that break his pipelines.
>
> Leah is an analytics engineer building dbt pipelines. She takes requirements from data analysts and builds datasets to meet those requirements. She struggles to find the data she wants and needs to learn a lot about the upstream services and their data models in order to produce what she hopes is the right data. These dbt pipelines now number in the thousands and no one has all the context required to debug them all. The pipelines break regularly, and those breakages often have a wide impact.
>
> The BI analyst, Bukayo, takes this data and creates reports to support the business. They often break due to an issue upstream. There are *no expectations* defined at any of these steps, and therefore *no guarantees on the reliability or correctness of the data* can be provided to those consuming Bukayo's data.
>
> The data generator, Vivianne, is far away from the data consumer, Bukayo, and there is no communication. Vivianne has no understanding or visibility of how the changes she makes affect key business processes.
>
> While Bukayo and his peers can usually get the data they need prioritized by Leah and Ben, those who are not BI analysts and want data for other needs have access to the data in a structured form, but lack the domain knowledge to use it effectively. They *lack the autonomy* to ask for the data they need to meet their requirements.

So, despite the improvements in the technology and architecture over three generations of data platform architectures, we *still* have that bottleneck of a central team with a long backlog of datasets to make available to the organization before we can start using it to drive business value.

The following diagram shows the three generations side by side, with the same bottleneck highlighted in each:

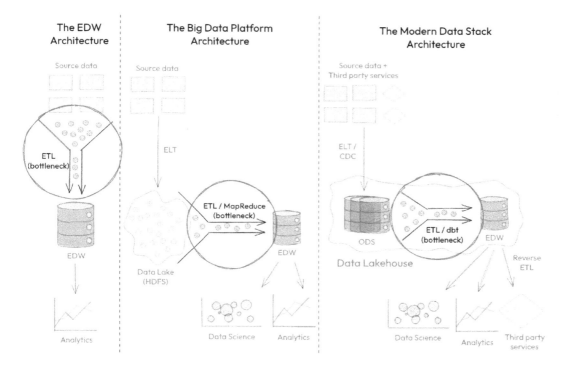

Figure 1.4 – Comparing the three generations of data platform architectures

It's that bottleneck that has led us to the state of today's data platforms and the trouble many of us face when trying to generate business value from our data. In the next section, we're going to discuss the problems we have when we build data platforms on this architecture.

The state of today's data platforms

The limitations of today's data architectures, and the data culture they reinforce, result in several problems that are felt almost universally by organizations trying to get value from their data. Let's explore the following problems in turn and the impact they have:

- The lack of expectations
- The lack of reliability
- The lack of autonomy

The lack of expectations

Users working with source data that has been ingested through an ELT or CDC tool can have very few expectations about what the data is, how it should be used, and how reliable it will be. They also don't know exactly where this data comes from, who generated it, and how it might change in the future.

In the absence of explicitly defined expectations, users tend to make assumptions that are more optimistic than reality, particularly when it comes to the reliability and availability of the data. This only increases the impact when there is a breaking change in the upstream data, or when that data proves to be unreliable.

It also leads to the data not being used correctly. For example, there could be different tables and columns that relate to the various dimensions around how a customer is billed for their use of the company's products, and this will evolve over time. The data consumer will need to know that in detail if they are to use this data to produce revenue numbers for the organization. They therefore need to gain in-depth knowledge of the service and the logic it uses so they can reimplement that in their ETL.

Successfully building applications and services on top of the data in our lakehouse would require the active transfusion of this knowledge from the upstream data generators to the downstream data consumers, including the following:

- The domain models the dataset describes
- The change history of the dataset
- The schematics and metadata

However, due to the distance between these groups, there is no feasible way to establish this exchange.

This lack of expectations, and no requirement to fulfill them, is also a problem for the data generators. Often, they don't even know they are data generators, as they are just writing data to their internal models in their services database or managing a third-party service as best they can to meet their direct users requirements. They are completely unaware of the ELT/CDC processes running to extract their data and its importance to the rest of the organization. This makes it difficult to hold them responsible for the changes they make and their downstream impact, as it is completely invisible to them and often completely unexpected. So, *the responsibility falls entirely on the data teams* attempting to make use of this data.

This lack of responsibility is shown in the following diagram, which is the same as we saw in the *The modern data stack* section earlier but annotated with responsibility.

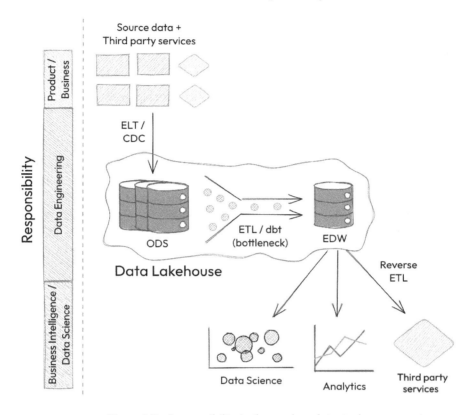

Figure 1.5 – Responsibility in the modern data stack

This diagram also illustrates another of the big problems with today's data platforms, which is the complete *lack of collaboration* between the data generators and the data consumers. The data generators are far removed from the consumption points and have little to no idea of who is consuming their data, why they need the data, and the important business processes and outcomes that are driven by that data. On the other side, the data consumers don't even know who is generating the data they depend on so much and have no say in what that data should look like in order to meet their requirements. They simply get the data they are given.

The lack of reliability

Many organizations suffer from unreliable data pipelines and have done for years. This could be at a significant cost, with a Gartner survey (`https://www.gartner.com/smarterwithgartner/how-to-stop-data-quality-undermining-your-business`) suggesting these cost companies millions of dollars a year.

There are many reasons for this unreliability. It could be the lack of quality of the data when ingested, or how the quality of that data has degraded over time as it becomes stale. Or the data could be late or incomplete.

The root cause of so many of these reliability problems is that we are building on *data that was not made for consumption*.

As mentioned earlier, data being ingested through ELT and CDC tools can change at any time, without warning. These could be schema changes, which typically cause the downstream pipelines to fail *loudly* with no new data being ingested or populated until the issue has been resolved. It could also be a change to the data itself, or the logic required to use that data correctly. These are often *silent* failures and may not be automatically detected. The first time we might hear about the issue is when a user brings up some data, maybe as part of a presentation or a meeting, and notices it doesn't look quite right or looks different to how it did yesterday.

Often, these changes can't be fixed in the source system. They were made for a good reason and have already been deployed to production. That leaves the data pipeline authors to implement a fix within the pipeline, which in the best case is just pointing to another column but more likely ends up being yet another `CASE` statement with logic to handle the change, or another `IFNULL` statement, or `IF DATE < x THEN do this ELSE do that`. This builds and builds over time, creating ever more complex and brittle data pipelines, and further increasing their unreliability.

All the while, we're increasing the number of applications built on this data and adding more and more complexity to these pipelines, which again further increases the unreliability.

The cost of these reliability issues is that *users lose trust in the data*, and once that trust is lost it's very hard to win back.

The lack of autonomy

For decades we've been creating our data platforms with a bottleneck in the middle. The team, typically a central data engineering or BI engineering team, are the only ones who have the ability and the time to attempt to make use of the raw source data, with everyone else consuming their data.

Anyone wanting to have data made available to them will be waiting for that central team to prioritize that ask, with their ticket sitting in a backlog. These central teams will never have the capacity to keep up with these requests and instead can only focus on those deemed the highest priority, which are typically those data sources that drive the company KPIs and other top-level metrics.

That's not to say the rest of the data does not have value! As we'll discuss in the following section, it does, and there will be plenty of ways that data could be used to drive decisions or improve data-driven products across the organization. But this data is simply *not accessible* enough to the people who could make use of this data and therefore sits unused.

To empower a truly data-driven organization, we need to move away from the dependence on a central and limited data engineering team to an architecture that promotes autonomy, opening that dark data up to uses that will never be important enough to prioritize, but that when added up provide a lot of business value to the organization and support new applications that could be critical for its success.

This isn't a technical limitation. Modern data lakehouses can be queried by anyone who knows SQL, and any data available in the lakehouse can be made available to any reporting tool for use by less technical users. It's a limitation of the way we have chosen to ingest data through ELT, the lack of quality of that data, and the data culture that embodies.

As we'll discuss in the next section, organizations are looking to gain a competitive advantage with the ever-increasing use of data in more and more business-critical applications. These limitations in our data architecture are no longer acceptable.

The ever-increasing use of data in business-critical applications

Despite all these challenges, data produced on a data platform is being increasingly used in business-critical applications.

This is for good reason! It's well accepted that organizations that make effective use of data can gain a real competitive advantage. Increasingly, these are not traditional tech companies but organizations across almost all industries, as technology and data become more important to their business. This has led to organizations investing heavily in areas such as data science, looking to gain similar competitive advantages (or at least, not get left behind!).

However, for these data projects to be successful, more of our data needs to be accessible to people across the organization. We can no longer just be using a small percentage of our data to provide top-level business metrics and nothing more.

This can be clearly seen in the consumer sector, where to be competitive you must be providing a state-of-the-art customer experience, and that requires the atomic use of data at every customer touchpoint. A report from McKinsey (https://www.mckinsey.com/industries/retail/our-insights/jumpstarting-value-creation-with-data-and-analytics-in-fashion-and-luxury) estimated that the 25 top-performing retailers were digital leaders. They are 83% more profitable and took over 90% of the sector's gains in market capitalization.

Many organizations are, of course, aware of this. An industry report by Anmut in 2021 (`https://www.anmut.co.uk/wp-content/uploads/2021/05/Amnut-DLR-May2021.pdf`) illustrated both the perceived importance of data to organizations and the problems they have utilizing it when it stated this in its executive summary:

> *We found that 91% of business leaders say data's critical to their business success, 76% are investing in business transformation around data, and two-thirds of boards say data is a material asset.*
>
> *Yet, just 34% of businesses manage data assets with the same discipline as other assets, and these businesses are reaping the rewards. This 34% spend most of their data investment creating value, while the rest spend nearly half of their budget fixing data.*

It's this lack of *discipline* in managing their data assets that is really harming organizations. It manifests itself in the lack of expectations throughout the pipeline and then permeates throughout the entire data platform and into those datasets within the data warehouse, which themselves also have ill-defined expectations for its downstream users or data-driven products.

The following diagram shows a typical data pipeline and how at each stage the lack of defined expectations ultimately results in the consumers losing trust in business-critical data-driven products:

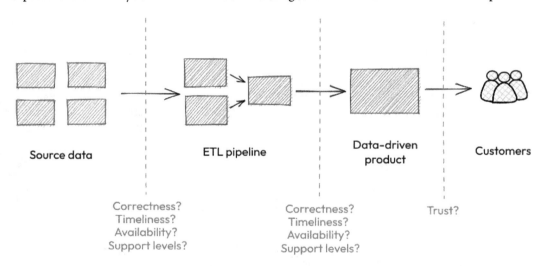

Figure 1.6 – The lack of expectations throughout the data platform

Again, in the absence of these expectations, users will optimistically assume the data is more reliable than it is, but now it's not just internal KPIs and reporting that are affected by the inevitable downtime but revenue-generating services affecting external customers. Just like internal users, they will start losing trust, but this time they are losing trust in the product and the company, which can eventually cause real damage to the company's brand and reputation.

As the importance of data continues to increase and it finds its way into more business-critical applications, it becomes *imperative* that we greatly increase the reliability of our data platforms to meet the expectations of our users.

Summary

There's no doubt that the effective use of data is becoming ever more critical to organizations. No longer is it only expected to drive internal reporting and KPIs, but the use of data is driving key products both internally and externally to customers.

However, while the tools we have available are better than ever, the architecture of the data platforms that underpin all of this have not evolved alongside them. Our data platforms continue to be hampered by a *bottleneck* that restricts the accessibility of the data. They are unable to provide the reliable, quality data that is needed to those teams who need it when it is needed.

We need to stop working around these problems within the data platform and address them *at the source*.

We need an architecture that *sets expectations* around what data is provided, how to use it, and how reliable it will be.

We need a data culture that treats data as a first-class citizen, where *responsibility is assigned* to those who generate the data.

And so, in the next chapter, we'll introduce **data contracts**, a new architecture pattern designed to solve these problems, and provide the foundations we need to empower true data-driven organizations that *realize the value* of their data.

Further reading

For more information on the topics covered in this chapter, please see the following resources:

- *From Data Warehouse to Data Lakehouse: The Evolution of Data Analytics Platforms* by Henry Golas: `https://cloudian.com/blog/from-data-warehouse-to-data-lakehouse-the-evolution-of-data-analytics-platforms/`

- *The Rise of ELT for DW Data Integration* by Chris Tabb: `https://www.leit-data.com/the-rise-of-elt-for-dw-data-integration/`

- *The Modern Data Stack: Past, Present, and Future* by Tristan Handy: `https://www.getdbt.com/blog/future-of-the-modern-data-stack/`

- *DBLog: A Generic Change-Data-Capture Framework*: `https://netflixtechblog.com/dblog-a-generic-change-data-capture-framework-69351fb9099b`

- *Capturing Data Evolution in a Service-Oriented Architecture* by Jad Abi-Samra on the Airbnb Tech Blog: `https://medium.com/airbnb-engineering/capturing-data-evolution-in-a-service-oriented-architecture-72f7c643ee6f`

- *Data Systems Tend Towards Production* by Ian Macomber: `https://ian-macomber.medium.com/data-systems-tend-towards-production-be5a86f65561`

- *How Netflix used big data and analytics to generate billions* by Michael Dixon: `https://seleritysas.com/blog/2019/04/05/how-netflix-used-big-data-and-analytics-to-generate-billions/`

- *How Uber uses data science to reinvent transportation?* ProjectPro: `https://www.projectpro.io/article/how-uber-uses-data-science-to-reinvent-transportation/290`

- *How DoorDash built the greatest go-to-market playbook ever* by Lars Kamp: `https://findingdistribution.substack.com/p/how-doordash-built-the-greatest-go`

- *Why Retailers Fail to Adopt Advanced Data Analytics* by Nicole DeHoratius, Andrés Musalem, and Robert Rooderkerk: `https://hbr.org/2023/02/why-retailers-fail-to-adopt-advanced-data-analytics`

- *Companies are losing revenue opportunities and customers because of bad data practices* by Bob Violino: `https://www.zdnet.com/article/companies-are-losing-revenue-opportunities-and-customers-because-of-bad-data-practices/`

2
Introducing Data Contracts

In the previous chapter, we looked at the problems we need to solve, and why it requires a new kind of data architecture. In this chapter, we'll introduce data contracts as our solution. We'll provide a definition and explore exactly what it is and how it solves those problems.

One of the best analogies for data contracts is that they act as APIs for your data. That sounds simple, but it's a fundamental change in how we build our data architecture. As we'll see later in this chapter, by thinking about providing an API for data, you'll start defining expectations around that API and consider the ownership and responsibilities. People often refer to an API as a *contract* between the provider and consumer, and it's that idea that eventually led to me calling them **data contracts**.

But an API is just one example of an **interface**, and really, it's interfaces that are the key to designing and implementing an architecture that defines the right expectations, builds in reliability, and promotes autonomy.

After building a shared understanding of data contracts, we'll consider when you should adopt data contracts, and discuss the types of organizations most ready for and best suited to applying data contracts to solve their problems.

Finally, in this chapter, we will discuss how data contracts relate to **data mesh**, another concept that aims to solve many of the same problems we want to solve with data contracts, and one of the inspirations for data contracts. We'll look at how they align, where they differ, and how data contracts can be used as a step toward a full data mesh (or maybe, they might be all you need!).

After reading this chapter, you'll have a solid understanding of data contracts, what they are, and how they solve the universal problems of today's data architectures.

In this chapter, we're going to cover the following main topics:

- What is a data contract?
- When to use data contracts
- Data contracts and the data mesh

What is a data contract?

We'll start by defining what a data contract is and break down that definition to explore the key principles that make up a data contract. Having an agreed definition will then allow us to understand how data contracts solve the problems we described in *Chapter 1, A Brief History of Data Platforms*, and give us the foundations we need in the later chapters as we look at exactly how to build and deploy an architecture built on data contracts – one that ultimately changes our data culture and allows us to extract the most business value from our data.

So, let's start with a definition. I define a data contract as follows:

A data contract is an agreed **interface** *between the generators of data and its consumers. It sets the* **expectations** *around that data, defines how it should be* **governed***, and facilitates the* **explicit** *generation of quality data that meets the business requirements.*

Those four keywords highlighted are the four key *principles* that data contracts are built on. We'll discuss these in more detail in the following sections:

- An agreed *interface* between the generators of data, and its consumers
- Setting *expectations* around that data
- Defining how the data should be *governed*
- Facilitating the *explicit* generation of quality data

> **Note**
>
> Throughout this book, we'll mostly be talking about applying data contracts to data your organization generates internally. This is the most important data to an organization, and therefore the data we need to make available to the business at the right quality. It's also the data we have the most ability to change and improve.
>
> There will be important data whose generation we have little control over, for example, data we ingest from third parties such as Salesforce or a partner's API. We can still apply many of the same *principles* of data contracts to those datasets.
>
> For example, we can have a conversation with our Salesforce admins and developers about the data we need, the format we need it in, how to handle migrations when that data changes, and so on. We could write that in a document, and that's a data contract. We could codify these rules in a tool such as Great Expectations (https://greatexpectations.io/) or Soda (https://www.soda.io) and assign responsibility for any breakages to those admins.
>
> For a partner whose API we depend on, that API can start to include data quality rules that they take responsibility for. We may even be able to start talking about data quality as part of the legal agreement we have with them, in the same we talk about their performance and dependability as part of **service-level agreements** (**SLAs**).
>
> So, while it's not the focus of this book, the principles of data contracts can certainly be applied to third-party data.

An agreed interface between the generators of data, and its consumers

Interfaces are the key to any architecture where we want to allow consumers to have confidence in their dependencies, which is why you see interfaces everywhere in software.

Consider when you import a third-party library into your code. That provides a well-documented interface in the way of public methods that you know you can rely on and use with confidence. That interface may evolve over time, and if so, a new version will be released. If it's a breaking change, that would be made clear by there being a release of a new major version, and there will be a migration path from the old version to the new.

There are often ways you can avoid the public interface and call the private methods, and maybe that's what you feel you need to do in order to meet your requirements. However, you can have no expectations that this method will continue to be supported from one version to the next. If/when it does break, that breakage is your responsibility, not the provider of the library.

Another great example of an interface in software is an API. These are of course used everywhere, both within organizations and between organizations, and as with software libraries are typically versioned, documented, and well-supported.

Within organizations, many have been building out **service-orientated architectures** (**SOAs**) or micro-service architectures for decades, which aim to reduce the coupling between different parts of a product or service that are owned and operated by different teams in order to improve developer speed, service resilience, and scalability. Interfaces underpin this in much the same way as they did for code libraries, although that interface also needs to set expectations around the performance of the service, its **service-level objectives** (**SLOs**), and support levels.

Sometimes these interfaces are taken further and become an industry standard that specifies exactly what the format should be. For example, ISO 8583 is an international standard that defines the format and protocol for exchanging financial transaction messages between different financial institutions. As with the other interfaces we've discussed, the standard is versioned. There have been several revisions released since the initial version in 1987 as the standard has evolved, ensuring it is still relevant and widely used today.

As well as providing a well-documented and supported foundation consumers can build upon with confidence, interfaces also provide an *abstraction* that hides the implementation details of the component. This decoupling allows the providers of the interface to make changes to that implementation quickly and with autonomy, knowing they won't be impacting their consumers.

Furthermore, the creation of an interface naturally brings the providers and the consumers closer together as they come to an *agreement* on the structure and the expectations of that interface. The consumer can discuss their requirements and share the context of why they need this interface and the value they can build from it. With this understanding, the provider is more incentivized to provide a quality interface that meets their requirements and gains a sense of ownership of the business value they are helping to create.

While the benefits of using interfaces are clear, there is of course a cost to building these interfaces. This cost can be significantly reduced with the right tooling and support. For example, most modern frameworks and libraries provide tools and utilities that simplify API development, including the definition of the endpoints, error handling, the generation of client libraries, and the publishing of documentation. There are also many resources and standards that help providers design an easy-to-use API, including RFC 9110 for HTTP semantics (`https://www.rfc-editor.org/rfc/rfc9110`) and semantic versioning for the consistent use of version numbers (`https://semver.org`). We can provide the same quality of tooling for data contacts, as we'll discuss in *Chapter 7, A Contract-Driven Data Architecture*.

This is why interfaces are a key part of data contracts. Data consumers – just like teams and organizations that consume and build upon APIs and standards – need an interface around the data they consume if they are going to build their analytics, models, and data products on that data with *confidence*.

We'll be talking more about expectations in the following section, as it's the next principle of data contracts.

Setting expectations around that data

Once we have an interface, we can use that to set the *expectations* around the data. It's these expectations that define how to use the data, what the structure of the data is, and how performant the data will be.

Without having well-defined expectations for the data you depend on, you can't set realistic expectations for your downstream users of the data product you are building. For example, if you don't know how timely the data will be, you can't confidently tell your users when to expect the latest data for their analysis.

A data contract can set the following expectations around the data, which we will be discussing in turn:

- The structure/schema of the data
- The valid/invalid data values (data quality checks)
- How performant and dependable the data is (via SLOs)
- Ownership and responsibilities

The structure/schema of the data

To make use of any data, you need to know what the structure of the data is. This is typically defined in a **schema**.

Schemas are of course nothing new. A relational database has a well-defined schema. There are a plethora of **Interface Definition Languages** (**IDLs**) that can be used to define schemas for serialized data, including protocol buffers (a.k.a., protobuf), Apache Thrift, and Apache Avro. There's also JSON Schema for defining a schema over JSON documents, upon which standards such as OpenAPI and AsyncAPI are built.

Alternatively, you could define your schemas in some custom or abstract format, for example in YAML or JSON, or even in code such as Python. This can give you more flexibility at the cost of interoperability.

We'll be looking in detail at how to define a schema in *Chapter 6, What Makes Up a Data Contract*. These schemas define exactly what the structure of the data is, which at least should include the following:

- The name and data type of each field available

- Documentation for those fields describing their purpose and limitations

Some of these formats can also be extended to include more useful information on the structure of the data that can be useful to consumers, including the following:

- The primary key(s)

- Data quality rules, for example, a valid range of values

- What entity the data relates to (for example, is it about a customer, an order, etc.?)

- Semantics (for example, units of measure)

- Whether it is personal data, and if so, is it identifiable (PII)?

- How the data is classified according to your organization's policies (for example, is it confidential, secret, or public knowledge?)

This is not an exhaustive list, and what you need to define in your schema will depend a lot on the kind of data it is and the organization implementing data contracts. But data contracts do provide a great place to define this metadata for use not just by consumers but also by other tooling, as we'll explore later in this chapter.

The valid/invalid data values (data quality checks)

The schema sets some expectations for what values a field can contain. For example, if the data type is a number, you know you will receive a number, and if it's a string you know it will be a string. However, what is a valid string for that field? How long can it be? Is there a limited number of allowed values, or any? Does it always conform to a particular format, such as an email address?

Knowing these make it a lot easier to work with the data and present it to the end users. For example, knowing a field named country_code will always be one of the few countries your business operates in, represented in the ISO 3166 format, allows you to decide how best to present that data. As a limited number of values, you know it will be fine to use as a dimension in a chart. If you wanted to present the country in the full form, you know how to perform that lookup.

Other data quality checks that could be implemented include the following:

- Minimum and/or maximum values for numbers

- Matches a defined standard, for example, a phone number or IP address

- Contains unique values only

- Matches a regular expression

- Referential integrity checks, for example, if the value of one field is x, there must be a value in another field

Capturing these validations in the data contract makes it clear that the data generator is responsible for producing data that passes those validations, and if not, it would breach the agreement they made with their consumers.

It also allows the data generators to incorporate these validations in their code. They can use them as part of their test suite, helping ensure the code they write produces valid data. They can also use them in production and catch invalid data before it is sent downstream, limiting the impact of the issue and alerting the data generator instantly to the problem so they can fix it as soon as possible.

We'll be showing how to define these validations in a data contract and how to use them to build libraries for data generators to use in *Chapter 8, A Sample Implementation*.

We now know *what* to expect from our data based on the schema and the valid data values. Next, we'll look at *when* to expect that data and whether we can depend on it for our use case.

How performant and dependable the data is (via SLOs)

Having expectations around the structure and the quality of the data helps us use the data, but to build on it with confidence we also need to know about the *performance* and the *dependability* of the data.

How performant and dependable the data needs to be depends on your requirements. For many use cases, the data doesn't need to be highly dependable, and therefore no further effort should be spent increasing its dependability. In other cases, for example, if your organization is using this data to provide a data-driven product to its customers, or if the data is required to accurately bill its customers, the dependability requirements increase.

When it comes to data, its performance and dependability can be measured in several ways. Three of the most useful measures are *completeness*, *timeliness*, and *availability*, as shown in the following diagram:

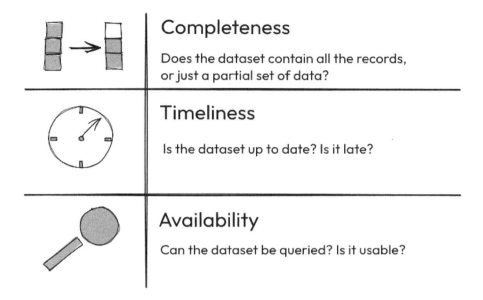

Completeness

Does the dataset contain all the records, or just a partial set of data?

Timeliness

Is the dataset up to date? Is it late?

Availability

Can the dataset be queried? Is it usable?

Figure 2.1 – Data performance and dependability measures

These are examples of **service-level indicators** (**SLIs**), which are direct measurements taken on your system that tells you how it is performing from a user's experience. They should be measured constantly with alerts raised instantly for the data generator when they indicate something is unhealthy.

From these measurements, you can create **service-level objectives** (**SLOs**). These are expressed as a percentage over time and define the expectations the data consumers can expect.

For example, we could measure the timeliness of our data by recording the difference in time between when the record was created, and when it was available for querying by the consumers. We could then set an SLO that the oldest available record is no older than (say) 1 hour. The data consumers now know how timely the data is expected to be and can make an informed choice on whether it meets their needs, and if it does what promises to make to their own users or consumers.

Unless you know what to expect from your data generators (and any other dependencies you have), you can't set expectations for your consumers. So, typically, they will assume your product or service is more performant and dependable than it really is. When that turns out not to be true and the data users start to lose *trust* in the data, once that trust is lost it is very difficult to win back.

We've implicitly been implying that this is the responsibility of the data generator, as the owner of the data. But it's always better to be explicit, so let's look now at what the ownerships and responsibilities are around the data contract.

Ownership and responsibilities

Finally, an interface helps to define the ownership and responsibilities clearly and explicitly. As we discussed in the previous chapter, with today's data platforms almost all the responsibility falls on the data engineering teams and the data consumers, and very little is assigned to the data generators.

This is a big problem, as it is those data generators who have the most control over the completeness, timeliness, and availability of the data. They also have the most context on the data and know why it is shaped the way it is, how it might have been populated over time, and how it needs to evolve in the future.

With data contracts, we're asking data generators to take on more responsibility for the data they create. It's a *shift-left* of responsibility, so we can address the data quality and dependability issues earlier. It's *their data*, and they need to provide it in a way that meets the requirements of the data consumers, in order to help the organization as a whole meet its objectives.

But we're also giving data generators the autonomy to decide how best to do that. They own the data contract, they decide how best to provide the data in a structure that takes into account the requirements of the consumers but also considers the trade-offs on their side around how to provide that in a scalable and maintainable way.

They are also the ones setting the expectations around that data, and they will be held accountable to those expectations. This includes the schema, the semantics, and the valid data values. It also includes performance and dependability, as expressed as SLOs.

However, it is up to the data consumers to make a case for this data and why they need a certain level of performance and dependability. They need to be able to articulate the value of the data and the business goals they are supporting with this data.

Having an interface and defining these responsibilities helps bring the data generators and consumers much closer together. The generators can now clearly understand the importance and impact of their data, and the consumers can make the case for better-quality data.

A lot of this is part of the culture change we're promoting with data contracts, and we'll talk more about that in *Chapter 4, Bringing Data Consumers and Generators Closer Together.*

> **Consumer-driven contracts**
>
> What we've been describing so far are known as *producer-driven contracts*. They are created and owned by the producer (the data generators), as it is they who have control over how the data is generated. APIs, as we discussed in the *Interface* section earlier, are also producer-driven contracts.
>
> This is the only way to implement data contracts in a way that supports and drives a culture where data quality is the responsibility of the data generators.
>
> *Consumer-driven contracts* are contracts created and owned by the consumer and applied to the data produced by the generator. They are a pattern often used in testing, for example, using Pact (`https://pact.io`), and can be implemented on data using tools such as Great Expectations (`https://greatexpectations.io/`) or Soda (`https://www.soda.io`).
>
> This can be useful to implement on data you have little control over, for example, if it is coming from a third party. But with data contracts, we're focused more on data we can control, typically produced internally, where we do have the ability to change how that data is produced, both through the implementation of tooling and by changing our data culture.

In the following section, we'll look at the next principle of data contracts, which is around documentation and governance.

Defining how the data should be governed

Data governance includes the standards, policies, and processes that define how an organization's data is managed. It is becoming increasingly important to organizations as data quantity and complexity grows, the risks of data misuse increase, and regulators across the world take steps to define how personal data can and can't be handled.

As mentioned previously, in *Setting expectations around that data*, we can extend the data contract with metadata that helps describe what the data is. This includes several characteristics and classifications that can help with the governance of the data, including the following:

- Is the data related to a person? If so, is it a direct or an indirect identifier?

- How sensitive is this data? Is it confidential, secret, or public knowledge?

- Who can access this data? And for how long?

- What is the retention period for this data?

- How is this data expired? If it is to be anonymized, what's the anonymization strategy?

- How has this data been processed?

How important some of these are depends on your organization, the type of data you generate or collect, and the regulations in the territories you operate in. However, there is a clear direction of travel when it comes to privacy regulation, so even if you don't need to track many of these today, you may well need to track them tomorrow.

The best people to determine how the data should be categorized and labeled are the data generators. They have the most context on the data, know what it is, where it's come from, and – through data contracts – what use cases they are making this data available for.

This metadata that describes the data and its governance can be captured in the data contract. This ensures it is kept up to date, by those who own this data, as/when the data evolves.

We're treating the data contract as the *source of truth* for everything we need to know about that data. This is not just useful for consumers and other stakeholders as they discover and make use of the data, but if the contract is available in a machine-readable format, then it can also be made available to other tools and services, including privacy tooling, data catalogs, and other data governance tooling.

We'll talk more about how embedding governance in our data contracts enables a decentralized and more effective approach to managing our data, and how by collecting this in the data contract we can build tooling that automates our data governance processes, in *Chapter 5, Embedding Data Governance*.

In the next section, we'll look at the last of our principles, and how data contracts facilitate the explicit generation of quality data.

Facilitating the explicit generation of quality data

In *Chapter 1, A Brief History of Data Platforms*, we looked at how the data on our data platform is typically in a very raw form that has been extracted as is from the source system using an **extract, load, transform** (**ELT**) tool. For example, we might use **change data capture** (**CDC**) to export a copy of the database to an operational data store, or an ELT provider such as Fivetran or Stitch. We saw how that led to unreliable and expensive data pipelines and the creation of a bottleneck that prevented access to much of the data.

The root cause of this is that the data we are building on was *not built for consumption*. It was designed to meet the needs and requirements of the upstream service and how it needs to model the world and is optimized for the transactional database underpinning that service.

And so the final principle in our definition highlights how, with data contracts, we are moving away from accepting data in a raw form that has been generated as a side product of the upstream services, to data that has been deliberately and explicitly generated *for consumption*, meeting the consumers' requirements, and allowing us to effectively drive great business outcomes through the use of quality data.

To do this, we need to bring our data generators and consumers much closer together, and we use the data contract to facilitate this collaboration. It becomes the perfect place to discuss the data that might be missing or not in the right format, and any differences in the expectations set by the generators and what is required by the consumers.

For a data consumer to drive that discussion, they need to be able to articulate the value of the data to them and to the organization. This is important, as it connects the data generators to the ultimate outcome, incentivizes them to help us achieve that outcome, and gives them a sense of ownership and responsibility for that outcome. We'll be discussing this in more detail in *Chapter 3, How to Get Adoption in Your Organization.*

We also need to support the data generators by providing them with tooling that makes it easy to explicitly generate this data and make it available through a data contract-backed interface. This should include managing the resources that provide this interface, tools that help manage this data, and libraries and patterns to help publish this data from their services. For example, to replace the consistency guarantees provided by a CDC tool, you might need to make it easy to use publishing patterns such as *outbox* (`https://microservices.io/patterns/data/transactional-outbox.html`) or *listen to yourself* (`https://link.medium.com/8G6wGLjvSzb`). We'll explore how to support data generators in more detail in *Chapter 7, A Contract-Driven Data Architecture,* and the publishing patterns in *Chapter 10, Data Contracts in Practice.*

The four principles of data contracts

As we've seen, each of the four principles in our definition work together to drive a step change in building reliable, trusted, and effective data platforms, and help us achieve our aim of increasing the value our organizations can get from our data.

The data generators and the data consumers agree on an interface for the data that meets the business requirements and defines the expectations of that dataset and the governance around that dataset. It's through this interface that the data is explicitly made available to the consumers, decoupling them from the internal models of the upstream service to provide something they can build on with confidence.

In the next section, we'll discuss the concepts of data products, and how data contracts provide the interface for these products.

When to use data contracts

Now we have a good understanding of what data contracts are and how they solve the problems we saw in *Chapter 1, A Brief History of Data Platforms,* how do we know when is a good time to adopt data contracts in an organization?

Firstly, it depends on how your organization is using or wants to use its data. As discussed in the previous chapter, many organizations are starting to use data in more business-critical processes or in products they build for their customers. The ability to build these products quickly and effectively depends on the accessibility of easy-to-use, quality data, and data contracts help with the production of that data.

Then, once these data-driven applications are released, data contracts help ensure they stay performant and dependable by tracking the SLOs of the data and managing the evolution of that data, preventing breaking changes that impact downstream consumers.

Even if your organization is not ready to use data for critical use cases, if it is using data at all then the first thing the users of that data want to know is *"Can I rely on this?"*. They want to know whether it is correct, whether it is up to date, and whether it will be available when they need it. Above all, they favor the *stability* of that data application.

For these reasons, I believe data contracts are worth adopting early on and are not just something larger organizations will benefit from. The truth is, once you have product market fit, your core data models are fairly stable, so we're not really sacrificing our organization's velocity by adopting a more deliberate approach to data from the start.

To take GoCardless as an example, when I joined over 5 years ago, our core models were around payments, bank details, and so on. Since then, we've expanded into many countries around the world, started using open banking alongside direct debit to collect payments, and added new product offerings alongside our core product. And yet, the core models are not all that different. Of course, they've evolved and been extended, but at its core are still datasets describing payments, the amounts, the fees, the bank accounts those payments are between, and so on.

It's also true that the later you adopt it, the harder it will be. The existing data culture will be much more ingrained and it's going to take a lot of effort to change that. You will have legacy pipelines you will need to decommission and datasets that will need to be migrated to data contracts. It's not impossible, and we'll be providing plenty of advice in this book to help you! But it is harder.

If you are bringing data contracts into a larger organization, it is usually best to start with a few specific use cases. Take those data applications that are most critical for the business, and from there work back to improve the quality and dependability of the data they depend on. Measure the impact of this change, perhaps by looking at a reduction in data incidents, reduced ETL costs, or the speed of iteration on these products. Use these measurements to show the *value* in the move toward data contracts.

You can do this with minimal investment in tooling. The most basic data contract is a document describing the data, as agreed by the data generators and the data consumers. With just that, you've started bringing those groups together, increasing the understanding the data generators have of the problems faced by the consumers, and allowing the consumers to share their requirements and what they could do if the quality and accessibility of data was improved. Then iterate on the tooling you need to create more usable and enforceable data contracts as you work toward building your ideal data contract implementation.

We'll be discussing more about how to make the case for data contracts in *Chapter 3, How to Get Adoption in Your Organization*.

In the next section, we'll look at Data Mesh. This is a pattern also aiming to solve the problems we've been discussing throughout this book. We'll explore where they are similar, and where they differ.

Data contracts and the data mesh

Data mesh was invented by Zhamak Dehghani in 2019 (`https://martinfowler.com/articles/data-monolith-to-mesh.html`) and is a design pattern for building a domain-oriented, decentralized data platform. It focuses not just on the technology, but also the social and cultural changes required to achieve this goal and solve many of the problems we discussed in *Chapter 1, A Brief History of Data Platforms.*

The pattern is described through four principles:

- Domain ownership
- Data as a product
- Self-serve data platform
- Federated computational governance

Let's go through each principle in turn and discuss how they relate to data contracts.

Domain ownership

Data mesh proposes a domain-oriented approach to organizing the responsibility and ownership of the data, where this ownership is decentralized to the business domains closest to the data – ideally, the data generators. They are the ones who know most about the data and can change that data. It's *their data.*

Data contracts enable and promote domain ownership. They provide the interface where we can define this ownership, and related metadata such as the entity (or domain) that data relates to. It's also where the generators set the expectations around the data, which gives the data consumers the confidence to rely on this data.

With data contracts, we're encouraging data generators and data consumers to collaborate around this interface. The data consumers bring their requirements and describe why they need this data and the business value they want to create by building on this data. The data generators are then incentivized to produce quality data that meets those requirements.

Data contracts also promote domain ownership through the provision of tooling. That allows data generators in different domains to provide their data in the data warehouse, from where it can be made available to any other part of the business that needs it and joined with data from other domains. We'll be discussing this further in *Chapter 7, A Contract-Driven Data Architecture.*

It is essential that there is a well-defined interface at the boundaries of the domains – the boundaries of *ownership*. Data contracts provide that interface.

For domain owners to provide effective and easy-to-use data through these interfaces, they need to treat this data as a *product* they are providing to their consumers. This is the next principle of data mesh, which we'll look at next.

Data as a product

The principle of data as a product encourages the application of product thinking to our data. It promotes the generation of data that not only meets the needs of customers but also provides a great user experience from discovery to implementation.

As we discussed in *Chapter 1, A Brief History of Data Platforms*, most data is generated as a side product from the upstream services. One of the principles of data contracts is to move away from this to a model where we are deliberately and *explicitly* producing data products that meet the requirements of consumers.

These data products require an interface on them that defines the expectations around that data, the schema, the version, and how it evolves, and so on – all of which are key parts of a data contract, as we've been discussing throughout this chapter.

Then what you end up with is something that looks a bit like a *supply chain* of data products, where products depend on other products in order to add some value. Each of these products should be useful independently, and by having an interface with well-defined expectations, we can build up a chain of products without losing confidence in the pipeline. The following diagram shows this data supply chain in action, with data contracts as the interface for each, and how independently or combined they drive business value:

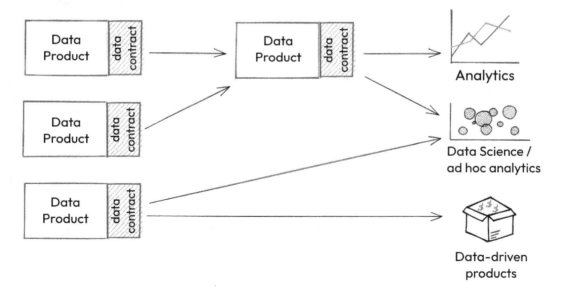

Figure 2.2 – Data products with data contracts as the interface

A strong case can be made that you don't have a data product if you don't have a data contract around it.

Data contracts also support the generation of data products through tooling, as we'll discuss in the next section.

Self-serve data platform

In order to enable the first two principles, we need to provide the teams working in their data domains the ability and autonomy to build their own data products through self-serve tooling.

This is important, as without providing standard tooling that enables the common use cases of these data generators, the effort required to produce quality data products is simply too high.

Through data contracts, we will be providing tooling that makes it easy for data generators to produce good-quality data that meets the requirements of their consumers. They'll be able to provide an interface to this data that is easy for them to write to, and easy for a consumer to read from. This tooling will be self-served and flexible, promoting the data generator's autonomy in designing and delivering their data products.

This is a big change for many centralized data engineering/platform teams. In fact, at GoCardless we explicitly changed the mission of our Data Infrastructure team to move away from *enabling GoCardless to make data-driven decisions, products, and services by providing a frictionless and trusted platform* to instead *providing best-in-class tooling so everyone can autonomously build reliable, scalable, and trusted data-driven products and services.*

We'll be discussing how to achieve this in detail in *Chapter 7, A Contract-Driven Data Architecture*, including making the case for a data infrastructure team to build and support this platform.

Federated computational governance

Data mesh is by design promoting a federated organizational structure, where domains have the autonomy to define their data products and the responsibility for them.

While the responsibility for governance is now shared across the organization, they still need to follow the standards and policies that have been set centrally. The proposal in data mesh is to utilize automation to help enforce these policies.

Data contracts provide the place where we can define the policies and provide the services that automate the enforcement of these policies.

For example, we discussed earlier, in *What is a data contract?*, how as part of the data contract, we can define whether the data relates to a person or not, whether it should be deleted or anonymized when we should no longer have that data, and what anonymization strategy to use. The responsibility for setting these definitions is assigned to the data generators, as they are the ones with the most context on this data, and they are supported by the standards, policies, and subject matter experts in the organization.

Once we have that definition, it's trivial to build tooling that can automate the expiry of that data when it exceeds its retention period, or in response to an action such as a deletion request from someone under the **General Data Protection Regulation (GDPR)**. That tooling will work no matter how the schema has been designed. If we have a standard way to define a contract, which includes the metadata that describes how we should manage the data, we can build common tooling to perform the required actions on that data, without requiring every data generator to become experts in privacy regulations.

We'll discuss more around how to embed data governance in data contracts in *Chapter 5, Embedding Data Governance,* and how we can build this kind of tooling on top of data contracts in *Chapter 7, A Contract-Driven Data Architecture.*

Data contracts enable a data mesh

As we have seen, there is a strong alignment between the goals and principles of data mesh and those of data contracts. In fact, data mesh was one of the inspirations behind data contracts. The articles came out around the same time I was thinking about solving the same problems and when I eventually came up with the concept. So, they should be considered complementary, rather than in competition.

What's missing from data mesh is how, exactly, you provide the tooling that enables the pattern and supports the organizational structures proposed. Data contracts fill that gap by providing an architecture that provides the interfaces where domain ownership is defined and the expectations around the data products are set, enabled through the delivery of a self-served data platform that automates data governance.

In fact, you probably cannot implement a data mesh without using data contracts.

However, data contracts are an important architectural component even if you're not attempting to implement a data mesh. You still need some interface to the data, and data contracts provide that. You still need somewhere to set expectations, including defining and implementing data quality checks. You still need to automate data governance and comply with current and future data regulations.

Just like you don't need to be building micro-services to benefit from good API patterns and tooling, you don't need to be implementing a data mesh to benefit from data contracts.

Summary

In this chapter, we introduced the concept of data contracts as our solution to the problems identified in *Chapter 1, A Brief History of Data Platforms.* We've provided a definition and discussed how data contracts provide an agreed *interface* between the generators of data and its consumers. That interface also sets the *expectations* around that data and how it should be *governed*. We then have everything we need to facilitate the explicit generation of quality data.

These are the *four principles* of data contracts, which work together to drive a step change in building reliable, trusted, and effective data platforms, and help us achieve our aim of increasing the value our organizations can get from our data.

By applying these principles, we are shifting the responsibilities *left*, moving more upstream to the data generators. We're addressing the data quality and dependability issues at source, by those who have the most knowledge of the data and the ability to change the data.

We also discussed when organizations should apply data contracts, why they should start as early as possible, and how to get started in a larger organization with an existing data culture.

Finally, we compared data contracts to data mesh, a design pattern and organizational framework that aims to solve many of the same problems, and how data contracts align with and enable the data mesh principles, but is ultimately an architectural pattern that brings benefits whether you are planning on implementing a data mesh or not.

In the next chapter, we'll start looking at how to adopt data contracts in your organization, by exploring the people and culture changes we need to facilitate alongside the changes in our technical architecture.

Further reading

For more information on the topics covered in this chapter, please see the following resources:

- *Building Highly Reliable Data Pipelines at Datadog* by Quentin Francois: `https://www.datadoghq.com/blog/engineering/highly-reliable-data-pipelines/`

- *Monte Carlo - The Rise Of Data Downtime* by Barr Moses: `https://www.montecarlodata.com/blog-the-rise-of-data-downtime/`

- *SRE fundamentals: SLI vs SLO vs SLA | Google Cloud Blog* by Adrian Hilton: `https://cloud.google.com/blog/products/devops-sre/sre-fundamentals-sli-vs-slo-vs-sla`

- *Data Processing Pipelines - Site Reliability Engineering*: `https://sre.google/workbook/data-processing/`

- *Should Your Data Warehouse Have an SLA? (Part 1) - Locally Optimistic* by Scott Breitenother: `https://locallyoptimistic.com/post/data-warehouse-sla-p1/`

- *Why Data Contracts are Obviously a Good Idea* by Yali Sassoon: `https://datacreation.substack.com/p/why-data-contracts-are-obviously`

- Dehghani, Z. (2022). *Data Mesh*. O'Reilly Media, Inc.

- *Data mesh – A Data Movement and Processing Platform @ Netflix*: `https://netflixtechblog.com/data-mesh-a-data-movement-and-processing-platform-netflix-1288bcab2873`

- *Data Contracts – ensure robustness in your data mesh architecture* by Piethein Strengholt: `https://towardsdatascience.com/data-contracts-ensure-robustness-in-your-data-mesh-architecture-69a3c38f07db`

- *Data Contracts: The Mesh Glue* by Luis Velasco: `https://towardsdatascience.com/data-contracts-the-mesh-glue-c1b533e2a664`

- *Building data products as a competitive differentiator* by Teresa Tung: `https://www.accenture.com/us-en/insights/technology/data-products`

Part 2: Driving Data Culture Change with Data Contracts

In this part, we'll focus on the culture change that is required as part of our adoption of data contracts, why it is so important to bring consumers and generators closer together, and how we can embed and automate data governance.

This part comprises the following chapters:

- *Chapter 3, How to Get Adoption in Your Organization*
- *Chapter 4, Bringing Data Consumers and Generators Closer Together*
- *Chapter 5, Embedding Data Governance*

3

How to Get Adoption in Your Organization

Now that we have a good understanding of what data contracts are and how they can help solve the data problems we have in our organizations, let's look at how we can get started on the journey toward implementing and deploying data contracts.

What we'll find is that while data contracts are a technical architecture supported by our tooling, they're also our vessel for *changing the data culture* in our organizations. We are moving away from data as a side product and instead applying more *discipline* to how we generate our data in order to meet the requirements of our data consumers. And we're doing that because we understand the value our organization can get from its data, and how that will lead to better outcomes for the business.

Changing the data culture is not easy but is essential for the successful adoption of data contracts. Throughout this chapter, we'll be discussing how to approach this culture change and providing actionable advice to help you get started.

By the end of this chapter, you'll be able to articulate the value of your data and unlock that value by building **data products**. We'll also walk through an example data product, showing how to apply these concepts in practice.

In this chapter, we're going to cover the following main topics:

- Using data contracts to change an organization
- Articulating the value of your data
- Building data products
- Walking through an example of a data product

Using data contracts to change an organization

We'll start by understanding how we can use the adoption of data contracts to change an organization. We'll learn about the two major roles involved in the extraction of value from data, and how they both need to change if we are to achieve our objectives.

It's important to keep in mind that data contracts are not just about implementing some tooling and defining a new architecture. If we want to make cultural changes, as we discussed in *Chapter 2, Introducing Data Contracts*, we need to change how *people* within the organization work with data.

In fact, I'd say data contracts are about affecting and facilitating this change in culture than the technology and how it is implemented.

There are two distinct roles we refer to in the context of data contracts:

- **Data generator**: The people generating data intended to be consumed by one or more data consumers. They often work in a product engineering team, and this data is typically generated by a service they support. They are the owners of this data.

- **Data consumer**: The people consuming this data. Often, we think of these as data practitioners, such as data engineers, business analysts, or data scientists, but often they are also software engineers, tech leads, or product managers who support a service that consumes data generated from another service and take action based on that data.

As we discussed in *Chapter 1, A Brief History of Data Platforms*, data generators often don't identify themselves as such, due to the way data is extracted from their databases and the little to no interaction they have with the data engineers maintaining these pipelines, let alone the data consumers.

And so, with data contracts, our data generators will feel they are taking on a new role. We are *empowering* them with greater autonomy and assigning them greater responsibility. We are showing them the value our organization gets from data and asking them to help enable it. Together with the data consumers, the data generators will now take some ownership, and some recognition, for those outcomes.

This will be a substantial change for them! Particularly if they are in a product team that is busy with other commitments, and now it sounds like they're being asked to do *more*. It may not even be clear *why* they should. That is why it's so important to have a strategy for culture change alongside your plans to roll out the new data architecture and the tooling around it.

You will need to be able to communicate the benefits of data contracts to data generators and other stakeholders at all levels and get their buy-in and sponsorship.

It's best to start this as early as possible and before any solution has been designed. You can present your ideas and get feedback from data generators on the direction you are considering taking. This early engagement will give them a sense of involvement and a feeling of ownership right from the start, and as the project develops, they will become your allies and help evangelize the approach and represent you and the data teams when you are not in the room.

As you do this, you're going to hear a lot of concerns. It's important to treat every concern as genuine and react with *empathy*, while being honest about what we're asking for and why we're doing this. This builds a strong relationship with the stakeholders, which will help get their buy-in.

But it's not just the data generators we are asking to change. We're also asking the data consumers to change.

They need to start asking for the data they need and being clear *why* they need it. This sounds easy, but after years of just accepting the data they're given, it's often a new skill they need to learn.

This is all part of how we start to bring the data generators and consumers much closer together, which we'll be covering in more detail in *Chapter 4, Bringing Data Consumers and Generators Closer Together*. They are *partners* who are working together to add value to their organization through the effective use of data.

Key to this is the ability of data consumers to effectively articulate the data they are providing to the business, which we'll be discussing in the next section.

Articulating the value of your data

Now, let's look at how to effectively articulate the value of your data, and why that is important as we adopt data contracts.

As we discussed in the previous section, we're explicitly asking the data generators to take on this new role and assigning them that responsibility. By doing this, we are moving the accountability for the quality of data left, upstream from the data engineers and their pipelines. This *shift-left* approach ensures data quality issues are addressed at source, by those who have the most knowledge of the data and the ability to change the data – the product teams.

If data consumers are going to ask our product teams to do more and incentivize them to do so, they need to be particularly good at articulating the value of our data, and the positive outcomes we are generating for the organization with that data.

This is *why* we are doing it. Why is it worth the investment in improving data quality? What are the positive outcomes we are generating for the business? Why are we investing in data instead of something else?

Without being clear on the why, we're not going to get data generators to adopt data contracts. Or even if they do, maybe because they are being mandated to by leadership, they're not going to be motivated to do it well and in line with the principles we discussed in *Chapter 2, Introducing Data Contracts*. It will just be the bare minimum to get it done.

How you articulate the value of data, and then data contracts, depends on who you are communicating with and how they are incentivized. If you're talking to the leaders in the organization, it's highly likely there are parts of the company-wide strategy that will only succeed with good-quality data.

Leaders are also most interested in how to make better decisions, and one way to do that is to use data to help them understand the past and the present and make predictions about the future.

Furthermore, there's a lot of value in making *faster* decisions. For example, using data and services built upon quality data to automatically take an action, either because it needs to happen in real time, or because to decide manually for thousands of cases isn't economical.

Your organization may also be investing in more data-driven products, particularly those driven by **machine learning (ML)**. If so, it should be quite easy to articulate the value of these investments, as those products will likely have revenue targets already associated with them.

Some of these things can be hard to measure in dollar terms, so instead I would suggest making these achievements more visible. There could be a regular newsletter highlighting a decision or business change that was driven by data. Or we could run presentations that show the data and how it tells a story about the performance of the business.

Either way, it's best to start with the business problem we're trying to solve with data and work back from there. You can rank these problems by criticality and value, then gradually roll data contracts out to other datasets as you prove the concept and develop your tooling.

How successful you are in articulating the value of your data will influence how you choose to roll out data contracts. It may be best to focus on a demonstrably high-value area first and prove the concept there. You can then use that as evidence of the impact of data contracts. For example, can you estimate the time it would have saved in creating that data-driven application had there been better quality data from the start? Is the resulting data-driven application more reliable and now achieving its **service-level objectives (SLOs)**? Is better or faster decision-making leading to more or higher-value sales?

Once we're clear on the value and how to communicate it, we can start asking for well-defined *data products*, supplying quality data, backed by data contracts.

We'll discuss moving your organization toward a data products approach and mindset more in the following section.

Building data products

As we discussed in *Chapter 1, A Brief History of Data Platforms*, most of the data made available to data teams is in tables and datasets extracted in raw form as is from source systems using an **extract, load, transform (ELT)** tool. That leads to unreliable and expensive data pipelines and the creation of a bottleneck where a central data engineering team effectively control access to any data of value.

With data contracts, we want to move away from thinking about the tables and datasets in the source system and instead start creating *data products*.

In the following sub-sections, we are going to cover the following:

- What is a data product?
- Adopting a data product mindset
- Designing a data product

What is a data product?

We introduced the concept of data products and the benefits of them in *Chapter 2, Introducing Data Contracts*. Let's go into more detail about the concept and define exactly what a data product *is*.

A data product is a high-quality dataset that has been designed for consumption by others. It aims to meet the requirements and expectations of those consumers and provide them with a dataset they can trust and build on with *confidence*. These expectations may include the setting of SLOs that the provider of the data product is accountable for meeting.

The data product may relate to one or more business entities (e.g., customers, orders), but should be scoped to a single business *domain*. That domain, and the teams within it, owns the data product and supplies it to the rest of the business.

Each data product has value on its own and can be used by anyone in the business looking to make use of data in their decision-making, processes, and applications.

Data products must be discoverable and accessible. They are provided through a well-defined, stable interface and include the necessary details needed to address that interface. They also include documentation on the fields and values of the data contained within the product and their meaning, semantics, and limitations.

Often, this discovery and accessibility is promoted through data catalogs and by surfacing the data lineage. We will discuss how data contracts help with data product discoverability in *Chapter 9, Implementing Data Contracts in Your Organization*.

The following diagram shows how these data products, with data contracts as the interface, drive the use of data in business applications. It also highlights how data products can be derived from other data products to combine data from different domains, building a *supply chain* of data products:

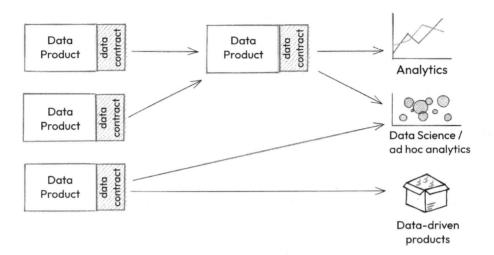

Figure 3.1 – Data products with data contracts as the interface

Data products should not be produced solely by central data teams. They should also be produced by those business domains that own the data. This promotes the *shift left* of data production, assigning responsibility for these data products to those who are the domain owners, who know most about the data and can change and improve and support it in the long term.

This shift left of responsibility is the key to removing the bottleneck we discussed in *Chapter 1, A Brief History of Data Platforms*, where the only accessible data is through the datasets produced by central data engineering and BI teams. By encouraging and supporting the creation of data products by all those who generate data, we're making accessible what was previously *dark data* and allowing anyone in the organization to build upon that data to drive business value.

The following diagram shows how the move to decentralized data products removes the bottleneck we had in our centralized data platforms and changes the assignment of responsibility. The data products are made available in our data lakehouse, having been explicitly produced by the source systems, and owned by the data generators within that domain. The interface for those data products is provided through data contracts:

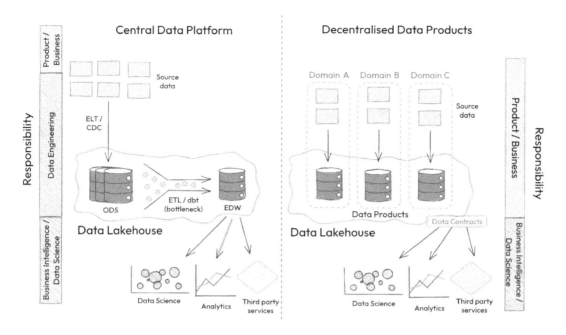

Figure 3.2 – The decentralized data products and the shift left of responsibility

Data products provide many benefits. They are more stable, accessible, and useful than datasets that have not been produced as a product. They encourage collaboration between the provider and the consumer, who work together as partners in the creation of business value using an organization's data. As the quality of the data increases, the time to insight and action is reduced.

There is also a reduction in costs, as data products provide the source of truth for data about a domain, with fewer duplicates created. Furthermore, any issues with that data are localized and the impact and cost of resolution are also reduced.

However, to create effective data products, we also need to adopt a data product mindset. Let's discuss that next.

Adopting a data product mindset

Now that we have a good understanding of what a data product is, let's explore how to create quality data products by applying a data product mindset.

A data product isn't all that different from any other product created by your organization. Of course, they're typically (but not always) for internal consumption. But applying product thinking to internal products is becoming increasingly common in other areas – for example, developer tooling – so your organization may already be familiar with the concept.

The first step is to understand why we need a data product. Who is it for? What are their requirements and expectations? This is another example of how data products, and data contracts, facilitate greater collaboration between data consumers and data generators. You can't build a great product without knowing who it is for.

The data consumers should have a good idea of the business needs they are looking to solve by building on this data product, and as discussed in the previous section, they will have been able to articulate that to the data generators. Knowing this, the data generators can appreciate the business value they are creating by providing this product, giving them a sense of ownership of that value.

These data products should be useful by themselves for driving data-driven applications and services, for example, dashboards and analytics, ML models, and internal or external services. They can also be sources for other data products and become part of a *supply chain* that builds value at each step.

As a principle, these supply chains should be kept as short and as efficient as possible. That reduces complexity and ensures no one team becomes a bottleneck in the use of our data. It also keeps the data generators close to the end consumers, so they can see the value of the data they create and feel ownership over the outcomes.

For example, if an engineering team can supply the data in the right format for a dashboard required by a finance team, they should feel empowered to do so, without needing permission or resources from a central data team. This is how we can remove those bottlenecks we discussed in *Chapter 1, A Brief History of Data Platforms*.

To aid with this shift in mindset, you may consider formalizing a *Data Product Manager* role, either as a full-time role or as part of an existing product manager role. They take responsibility for understanding the requirements of the data consumers and work with their product teams to meet those requirements. The core skill set of this role is much the same as any other product manager – they just need to learn about the different datasets their team owns and how the data products they build around those datasets unlock business value.

Now that we understand the data product mindset, in the next section, we'll look at how to design a data product.

Designing a data product

Let's discuss how to design a data product. This is a new skill for the data generators, who were previously detached from the data consumers and how they were using the data. They now need to learn how to design and build effective data products.

At an architectural level, we don't need to distinguish between who builds these data products. They could be engineering or data teams, depending on the product. What's important is that they are present at the *boundaries* of services, domain, or ownership, have a well-defined interface consumers can build on, and set the expectations around their dependability, performance, and support levels.

Knowing this, the data generators can start proposing a data contract. This will include the schema and some idea of the expectations around the data, for example, the suggested SLOs.

There will be several trade-offs the data generators make as they start working on the contract, including the following:

- What's the interface we will provide for this data? How will it be accessed?
- How does the production of this data impact their services and their performance?
- Can they produce this dataset at the expected scale, with the timeliness the consumers expect?
- Is this in a format they are happy to commit to supporting and keeping relatively stable?
- Does it have the flexibility to evolve as their services and the business evolves?
- Is the data sensitive, and if so, are the right controls in place around the data (for example, encryption, data minimization, and so on)?

This is why it's important that the *data generators own the contract* and have the autonomy to define it as they see it best. Only they have the required context to answer these questions and design a data product they are happy to support.

Data products should *not* be designed based on how the data is modeled and stored in the source system. That's internal to the service generating the data and is not necessarily a useful way of modeling the data outside of that system.

Instead, it should be related to a business entity and/or domain and be supplied to enable one or more known use cases.

Of course, a business evolves over time, and our data products will too. That's why we ensure our data contracts are *versioned*, with new versions being created as needed and a migration path that allows consumers to move to a newer version without any downtime or data loss.

But as discussed earlier, in *Chapter 2, Introducing Data Contracts*, our core data models do not change as often as you might think. Once your business has found its product market fit, the core models will be stable, even as your organization grows, and your product features expand. It's for this reason we can expect our data products to be stable, and our data consumers can build upon them with confidence.

Data products are an incredibly valuable way to think about how data is generated and how it's consumed. It's worth investing in data products early, particularly if they are around your core models or related to important business processes.

Over time, you'll find these products being applied to more use cases around the business, perhaps in combination with other data products, unlocking value you hadn't realized when you started. Furthermore, the more data that is available in the data product adds to its value and unlocks the ability to use that historical data in modeling and forecasting.

In the next section, we'll walk through a worked example of building a data product and put these ideas and concepts into practice.

Walking through an example of a data product

Let's work through a simple example that shows how to create a usable data product. This will solidify the ideas we've discussed so far in this chapter by applying them in practice.

Imagine we are building an e-commerce website that sells physical products directly to customers. We have many products and often apply discounts on these products as we react quickly to external factors in the market and internal factors such as our stock levels.

The way these discounts have been modeled and applied to orders has changed several times in the database that drives the service behind our e-commerce service. Initially, we added another field to the `products` table, but that meant a particular discount could only apply to a specific product, rather than many.

It was then extracted out to a new `discounts` table, which provided more flexibility in how we applied discounts across our product lines. However, the data was never backfilled in that table and the old column is still in the `products` table.

That gives us a database schema as shown in the following diagram. To keep things simple, we'll ignore other tables that would likely be present, such as the `customers` table:

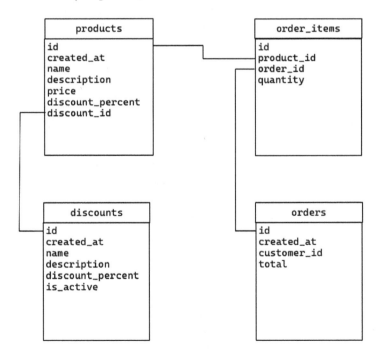

Figure 3.3 – Database schema for our e-commerce site

We're currently extracting that data through a **change data capture** (CDC) tool that recreates the data in our data lakehouse. It has the same structure, the same schema, and the same data. From there, the data consumers perform our ETL to convert this data into something that meets the requirements of their users.

In the future, the data generators are considering linking discounts to the order instead of the product as we look to personalize the discounts applied to our customers. That's something that's worrying our data consumers, as it could mean a substantial change in the underlying data models.

This discount data has a lot of *value* to the business. It's by looking at the performance of past discounts that the sales team decides what discounts to offer in the future, how much stock we will need in place, how best to market these discounts, and so on. We might even have a team of data scientists trying to model the expected impact of offering a discount, to help support the sales team in making those decisions.

Ultimately, it's the sales performance that matters most to the business and drives our revenue, and the effective use of discounts can drive a competitive advantage. And yet, despite that, the data is of *poor quality* and difficult to use.

As a consumer, you've had to encode a lot of business logic in your data pipelines. You have several CASE and IFNULL statements that change the logic based on the values, or absence of values. The SQL is now at over 800 lines and is expensive to run and hard to maintain.

You're not notified when the upstream logic changes and the first people to notice are your users, who don't understand why discounts seem to be missing from the dashboards or why they have been applied to some models and not others. They're starting to lose *trust* in this data.

Let's summarize the problems we're having with this approach based on building on top of the internal models of the database:

- Data generators need to be able to change the schema of their database, with autonomy, to deliver product features. We can't slow them down by having our data engineers review each change. So, we must accept regular schema changes.

- Our data pipelines are becoming ever more complex as we handle those changes. They are hard to reason with and we don't have confidence when making changes to those pipelines.

- That complexity is also further increasing the unreliability of the pipelines, and it takes longer to resolve those incidents.

- Users are losing trust in the data and are unsure whether they can rely on it.

- This lack of confidence prevents the effective use of this data. It's not being used to make decisions on discounts, leading to worse business performance.

So, how are we going to address these problems?

Thankfully, you and your colleagues have been reading this book! You have decided to move this to a dataset where a data product is provided, with an interface provided by a data contract. You have the right tooling in place to explicitly generate this data, and the culture has changed at the organization to one where data is treated as a first-class citizen, enabling us to extract the most value from our data to provide better outcomes for the business.

Moving to a data product aims to solve our problems as follows:

- The data generators explicitly supply data through a new interface. That decouples consumers from their internal models, allowing them to continue to make changes to their database quickly and with autonomy without affecting downstream consumers.

- The data provided through the data product meets the requirements of the consumers, reducing the amount of work needed in the data pipelines to make it useful. The transformations are simpler and easier to understand.

- The reduction in complexity increases the reliability of the data pipelines. When something does go wrong, it's easier to find and fix that problem.

- The data products set clear expectations on the performance and dependability of the data. The data engineers can also set similar expectations for their users. Those expectations allow users to trust the data.

- Users now have the confidence to use the data to support better decision-making, which leads to better business outcomes.

Let's look now at how we build this data product.

As we discussed earlier, in the *Adopting a product mindset* section, we should start with the data generators talking to the data consumers to understand their requirements. Once the data generators have a clear understanding of the requirements, they can define a schema for this data product.

This schema will be represented in the data contract. For this example, we will represent it as a YAML document, but we'll discuss the different ways to represent a data contract in *Chapter 6*, *What Makes Up a Data Contract*. As well as the schema, we will add an owner, a description, and a version to our data contract.

The following code snippet shows the data contract. For brevity, we haven't included all the fields here, but the full contract is available on GitHub at `Chapter03/order_events.yaml`:

```
description: An event generated when an order is created
owner: product-team@data-contracts.com
version: 1
fields:
  id:
    type: string
    description: The unique identifier for the order
```

```
created_at:
  type: timestamp
  description: The date and time the order was created
items:
  type: array
  fields:
    product_id:
      type: string
      description: The unique identifier for the product
    price:
      type: float
      description: The price of the product, in cents
    quantity:
      type: integer
      description: The amount of this product ordered
  ...
```

With this schema, represented in our data contract, we're now abstracted away from how discounts are modeled in the database. We don't have to maintain any logic downstream that determines whether to use the field in the `orders` table or the `discounts` table. We also don't have to keep that logic up to date when it changes again in the future. All we care about is the amount of discount applied to the item in the order, not how that discount is modeled in the upstream service.

We also agree to set expectations around this data. Currently, all decisions on discounts are made during the working day. It is useful to track how a discount is performing in close to real time, so if the sales team gets it wrong, they can quickly cancel the discount so as not to lose the business too much money. But this isn't critical to business performance in the same way as keeping the website up is, for example, and so neither is the availability of the data.

However, we do expect the order data to be complete. We don't want to have a mismatch between the orders in our system of record and those in our analytical database.

That leads to us defining the following SLOs for the data product:

- *Completeness*: The data will be 100% complete

- *Timeliness*: The data will be present within 60 minutes of being generated

- *Availability*: The data will be available for querying through the agreed interface 95% of the time

Of course, we could argue about the specifics of these SLOs, but the point is we've set the expectations and have agreement on them from the generators and consumers of the data. It's also been agreed that the interface for this product will be a table in the data lakehouse, from where it is consumed as a dashboard in a BI tool.

Let's add these SLOs and the location of the table to the data contract, as follows:

```
slos:
  completeness_percent: 100
  timeliness_mins: 60
  availability_percent: 95
lakehouse_path: order_events
```

Now that everything has been agreed upon by both the data generators and the data consumers and we have our data contract, the data generators get to work creating the dataset and start populating the data through the agreed interface. They also backfill the historical data, and this dataset becomes the source of truth for all consumers.

A lot of the complexity the data engineers had written into their data pipeline has been removed, and the pipeline is quicker and cheaper to run. The consumers are meeting their SLOs, and they are confident they will always be able to do so while the data generators meet theirs.

This schema is likely to be stable well into the future but could still change. If/when it does, the data generators now know who is consuming their data, and why this data is important for some key business processes. They will reach out to the consumers when that migration needs to happen and ensure there is a plan in place that prevents any impact on the business users.

This walk-through has been a relatively simple example, but one that illustrates how data products, backed by data contracts, change the way data is treated in an organization. By bringing the data generators and consumers closer together, they built a partnership toward the business goal. They set expectations, and now the data is more dependable and can be trusted by business users.

Later, in *Chapter 9, Implementing Data Contracts in Your Organization*, we'll provide more details on how to make the move to data products, backed by data contracts, in your organization.

Summary

In this chapter, we've started to see how data contracts are much more than a technical architecture with tooling to support it. They're a vessel for driving change in the data culture to one that invests in its data in order to deliver better business outcomes.

We introduced the two major roles involved, data generators and data consumers, and how they both need to change in order to achieve this goal.

Data consumers need to be clear about the value they can generate with data and why it's in the best interest of the organization to invest in quality data. We gave practical advice on how they can articulate the value of data.

Data generators need to buy into this and take on more ownership and responsibility for this data. They need to start building data products that meet the needs of the consumers and the wider organization.

We discussed exactly how they build these products and finished the chapter by walking through a simple example that showed these ideas in practice.

In the next chapter, we'll be building on these ideas and exploring how we can use them to bring data generators and consumers much closer together.

Further reading

For more information on the topics covered in this chapter, please see the following resources:

- Sinek, S. (2011). *Start With Why. Penguin*

- *Bring Product Thinking to Non-Product Teams* by Jeff Gothelf: `https://hbr.org/2020/04/bring-product-thinking-to-non-product-teams`

- *Manifesto for the Data-Informed* by Julie Zhuo: `https://joulee.medium.com/the-data-informed-manifesto-9dd8c240382f`

- *The importance of data quality for product-led companies* by Kevin Hu, PhD: `https://kevinzenghu.medium.com/the-importance-of-data-quality-for-product-led-companies-661d7d50d3b9`

- *Manage data like a product to unlock full value*: `https://www.mckinsey.com/capabilities/quantumblack/our-insights/how-to-unlock-the-full-value-of-data-manage-it-like-a-product`

- *Building Data Products for Data Transformation* by Teresa Tung: `https://www.accenture.com/th-en/insights/technology/data-products`

- *How to Build Great Data Products* by Emily Glassberg Sands: `https://hbr.org/2018/10/how-to-build-great-data-products`

- *What Is A Data Product And What Are The Key Characteristics?* by Sanjeev Mohan: `https://www.forbes.com/sites/forbesbusinesscouncil/2022/09/21/what-is-a-data-product-and-what-are-the-key-characteristics/`

- *How to identify Data Products? Welcome Data Product Flow* by P Platter: `https://medium.com/agile-lab-engineering/how-to-identify-data-products-welcome-data-product-flow-76d7d85d23af`

- *Build data products in a data mesh*: `https://cloud.google.com/architecture/build-data-products-data-mesh`

- *Why Your Company Needs Data-Product Managers*: `https://hbr.org/2022/10/why-your-company-needs-data-product-managers?ab=at_art_art_1x4_s03`

- *On Data Products and How to Describe Them* by Max Illis: `https://medium.com/@maxillis/on-data-products-and-how-to-describe-them-76ae1b7abda4`

4

Bringing Data Consumers and Generators Closer Together

In this chapter, we'll look at the importance of bringing data consumers and generators closer together and why that is one of the key objectives when adopting data contracts. It's only by being clear on the roles and responsibilities that these two groups of people can work effectively and efficiently to realize our goal of extracting the most business value from our data. Therefore, we'll start by defining these roles and what each of those roles expect from the other, before being explicit about the responsibilities and accountabilities of each role.

Next, we'll discuss a data consumer that is often overlooked – the product engineering teams. They are maybe the most important consumers in your organization and yet, like other consumers, are often unable to rely on the data that is generated. This leads to unreliable services or the inability to use the valuable data generated in other parts of the business.

Finally, we'll discuss how to support the evolution of your data as your organization itself evolves.

In this chapter, we'll cover the following main topics:

- Who is a consumer, and who is a generator?
- Assigning responsibility and accountability
- Feeding data back to the product teams
- Managing the evolution of data

Who is a consumer, and who is a generator?

We've spoken a lot about the consumers and generators of data in this book, but what exactly do people in these roles do? What do they care about? What are their requirements, and what are their expectations?

In the following subsections, we'll look at both roles in more detail, starting with the data consumers.

Data consumers

A data consumer is a person, a team, or a service that consumes data to inform and/or take some action. Typically, we think of data consumers as a data practitioner – for example, a data engineer, a BI analyst, or a data scientist. Their primary tasks require them to consume and work with data, and as such, they are highly reliant on the quality and dependability of that data.

However, they are not the only data consumers in your organization. There are an increasing number of people who are not data practitioners but are data literate. They are comfortable using a data analysis tool or another frontend (yes, including spreadsheets!) to consume the data themselves, helping them to perform a business process or support their decision-making.

Beyond people, both internal and external services are also data consumers. They take data as input and perform some tasks, or make a decision based on that data. Like all other data consumers, they too are reliant on the quality and dependability of the data. The only difference is that the services require a programmatic interface for the data, whereas people typically use a data analysis tool as their interface.

We can break these consumers down into different *personas*, each with their own requirements and data access patterns:

- *Software engineer (product team)*:

  - They integrate data into their service so that they can take some action on it. This can involve consuming data synchronously through an API call, or asynchronously by consuming from a message broker or event streaming platform.

  - Their data tends to be associated with a single business domain, either their own or an adjacent one.

  - Access patterns:

    - They may have low latency requirements

    - They need to be able to deserialize that data easily in their programming language of choice

- *Data scientist*:

  - They explore datasets to uncover patterns, correlations, and trends. Identifying and building features for use in their AI models. They typically use a notebook-based interface and access data in batches through a programming language such as Python.

  - They may work in a single domain on a specific product, or centrally across multiple domains.

  - Access patterns:

    - They need to understand the data and its context in detail

    - They often need access to historical data

- *Data/BI/analytics engineer*:

  - They join and transform data using an SQL-based tool, such as dbt (`https://www.getdbt.com/`), and provide this transformed data as a product to data analysts and/or business users

  - They can work within a single domain but often join data across domains

  - Access patterns:

    - Typically, they are not latency-sensitive and often run their transformations daily

    - They require a SQL-based interface

- *Data analysts and business users*:

  - They query curated data products through a BI tool or a spreadsheet-based interface, or within a service they already use. They use the data as part of a business process or to support decision-making.

  - They can be within a specific domain or look across multiple domains.

  - Access patterns:

    - They require the data to be available through their interface of choice

No matter which persona of data consumer they belong to, to be able to build on this data with *confidence*, they need to know what to expect from the data they consume.

Firstly, to make use of the data, they need to understand how it is structured and the fields that are available to them. That needs to be documented, to explain the meaning and context of that data and define the semantics. Depending on the data, this might also define whether it is personally identifiable, whether it is confidential or secret, what processing they are allowed to do with it, and other types of categorizations related to the compliance and governance of the data.

They then need to be clear about the dependability and performance of this data. This includes how timely the data is expected to be, how correct and how complete it is, and its availability. They also need to know who owns this data, and the support levels they provide.

Altogether, this forms the data contract.

While the data consumers do not own the data contract, they do play a major role in shaping that contract. They need to be able to articulate their requirements to the data generators and demonstrate the value they can generate through the application of data.

By providing quality data products through a data contract, we give the data consumers what they need so that they can work more effectively and deliver greater business value. They are then accountable for the delivery of that value.

Of course, many data consumers are also data generators – for example, a data engineer building a pipeline that transforms and combines data in order to meet the requirements of their consumers, or a service that takes data in, performs an action, and exports the result of that action. So, let's move to the next subsection and explore the role of the data generator.

Data generators

A data generator is a person or a service that generates data for later consumption. This may be an internal service that generates data as it runs or takes an action, a data pipeline that returns transformed or aggregated data, or a third-party service that provides us data as part of a commercial agreement.

As with the data consumers, we can break data generators down into personas:

- *Software engineer (product team)* :

  - They work on a service that generates data as the result of some action it has taken – for example, collecting an order from a customer or making a payment to a bank account. That data is needed by other teams and groups to build adjacent services and analyze business performance.

  - A service will usually belong to a single business domain.

- *Data/BI/analytics engineer*:

  - They build data products for consumption by data analysts and/or business users, meeting a specific requirement

  - They may work within a domain or across multiple domains

- *Third-party service*:

  - They typically make data available through an API. That API and/or the data it provides, and its dependability, may form part of a commercial agreement.

  - Some services may be specific to a single domain, and some may be used across domains.

In many organizations, the roles and responsibilities of data generators have not been well defined. In fact, those generating data might not even see themselves as data generators. As we discussed in *Chapter 1, A Brief History of Data Platforms*, this is because data was extracted from their systems with little to no involvement from them, and from then on, the process was owned by another team – typically, a data engineering or data platform team.

With data contracts, we are explicit about the role of the data generator and their responsibilities. It's they who know most about the data, and only they who can improve the quality and dependability of it.

By working closely with the consumers, data generators can gain a sense of ownership over the value they create and the positive outcomes for a business. This collaboration and knowledge sharing help incentivize the data generators to prioritize this work. Regular feedback from data consumers reinforces this further, and by recognizing the success of these projects and the role played by the data generators, we can foster and build on this data-driven culture, encouraging similar collaborations throughout the organization. We discussed this in more detail in *Chapter 3, How to Get Adoption in Your Organization*.

With this information, the data generator is empowered to provide the right data, with the right expectations, to meet the needs of their data consumers.

However, there are always trade-offs that data generators need to make. Consumers may prefer to have data in a particular format, but that could be expensive for the generator to provide. The consumers may ask for a particular level of performance, but the effort to meet that may be too high relative to the value. Generating this data may also impact the performance of the service they operate. So, a balance will need to be found between the requirements of the data consumers and what the data generators can provide.

This is why data generators must be the owner of the data contract. Only they can make decisions around these trade-offs, as only they have the full context. They need to be comfortable taking on the responsibility to generate this data and meet the expectations they commit to. It's the data generators who will support and maintain this data over the long term.

A data generator also has the responsibility to manage their data in line with their organization's policies. This could include categorizing the data, managing access, and ensuring the data is removed when it passes its retention period.

To support them in these tasks, they should have access to easy-to-use, self-served tooling. This should make it easy for them to do the right thing, without needing to become experts in data privacy and security, or, where possible, automate these tasks completely. Data contracts provide the foundations we need to provide this tooling, and we'll discuss what this should look like in *Chapter 7, A Contract-Driven Data Architecture*.

In the next section, we'll assign responsibility and accountability to both the data generators and the data consumers.

Assigning responsibility and accountability

Now that we have defined the roles, we need to specify the responsibilities and accountabilities of each role. This ensures that everyone knows what is expected of them and allows them to work most effectively together.

We'll start with the data generators. As we discussed in the previous section, many of them didn't realize they were data generators. Therefore, those responsibilities were taken by the data engineering team who built the pipelines that extracted the raw data from upstream services.

This data engineering team became accountable for the reliability of the data, even though they were not involved in how it was generated or how the structure of the data evolved. This team was very reactive to upstream changes and did their best to try and limit the impact of those changes. However, there is only so much they can do, and there's no quick fix you can deploy if the generator upstream suddenly stops writing the data you relied on.

We believe the only way to improve the quality and reliability of our data is to address how it is generated and be clear about the responsibilities of those who generate it.

This does mean these data generators will gain more responsibilities. If they are to accept that, they need to fully understand *why* they should do so. We discussed how to articulate that in *Chapter 3, How to Get Adoption in Your Organization*.

However, this is just a shift in the assignment of those responsibilities. They were already assigned, but to the data engineering teams. By shifting this responsibility *left* to the data generators, we put that responsibility on the team that has the most insight on why data is structured the way it is.

By assigning responsibility as early as possible, we are *proactive* in our approach to data quality. Only at the source can we be in complete control of the accuracy and dependability of data. If data is incorrect or missing from the source, it's going to be incorrect or missing from all downstream consumers. And if that issue cannot be resolved at the source, there's nothing we can do downstream to recover that data.

Shifting responsibility left also reduces the overall costs to the business. There will be fewer incidents caused by upstream data changes and a much-reduced impact from those incidents.

Over time, we can add more data quality checks at the source, moving them upstream from the data pipelines. This further reduces the risk and impact of data incidents and reinforces the assignment of responsibility to the data generators.

To take an example, we might have several data pipelines building upon the raw data model of an upstream service. The responsibility of those pipelines lies with the data engineering teams building those pipelines, but no one really has responsibility for the data generation.

When the expectations of the data changes, such as a schema change resulting in the generation of invalid data, each of those pipelines is affected. This is shown in the following diagram:

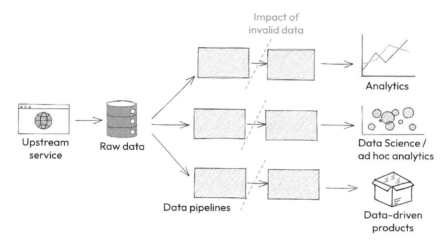

Figure 4.1 – The impact of invalid data when consuming raw data

This has an expensive impact because, now, each data pipeline needs to be updated to handle the change in data. That results in a duplication of code and effort that adds no value to an organization.

Instead, with data contracts, we provide an interface separated from the raw data. We also make clear that it is the responsibility of the data generator – in this case, the software engineers who own the upstream service – to provide data that conforms to that contract, and if not, they are accountable for fixing it. As shown in the following diagram, the impact is reduced:

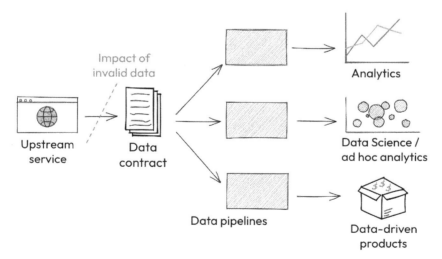

Figure 4.2 – The impact of invalid data when consuming from a data contract

The fix now only needs to happen in one place, and all downstream consumers benefit from it. Furthermore, as the data generators know this is part of their responsibility and are aware of the impact on their consumers, they will be more incentivized to prevent a similar incident from occurring in the future.

This shift left also means we can spend less time, effort, and money getting the data into the right shape in the data warehouse. Referring again to the previous diagrams, in *Figure 4.1*, each of those pipelines performs the same transformations and implements the same business logic. Alternatively, if we can move that earlier, as shown in *Figure 4.2*, it only needs to be done once, at the source.

We'll also be able to confidently set **service-level objectives** (**SLOs**) and other expectations in this data contract, building trust throughout the pipelines and the wider organization, and unlocking the use of data in business-critical applications. (We discussed SLOs and expectations in more detail in *Chapter 2, Introducing Data Contracts*, in the *Setting expectations around our data* section.)

And if the data generators understand why that data is important, they'll have the incentives to manage it with the care and discipline required to meet business goals.

This is where the data consumers responsibilities come in. If we're asking teams to invest in better quality and more reliable data, prioritizing it against other work they might be doing, we need our consumers to deliver impactful data products as a return on that investment.

It's well known that, today, many organizations struggle to see the returns on their investment in data. Despite that, they continue to invest, based on the assumption that there is value to be gained from their data. We believe we need to do better and hold our data consumers to account for the realization of the value we get from our data, and how that leads to greater outcomes for the business.

Data contracts provide us with the means to be more explicit about these responsibilities and accountabilities. Adopting data contracts is an opportunity to revisit our past assumptions and look again at how our data generates value for our organization. With data generators and data consumers working together, aided by clearly defined roles and responsibilities, we can more effectively deliver that value.

If we manage to achieve this, and we start generating quality data we can rely on, we can start to confidently use this data in different areas. For example, we can feed this data back to our product teams and use this data in business-critical applications that differentiate us in the market.

Let's explore this in more detail in the next section.

Feeding data back to the product teams

As mentioned earlier in this chapter in the *Who is a consumer, and who is a generator?* section, although we often think of a data consumer as a data practitioner (for example, a BI analyst or a data scientist), they're not the only ones who consume data. In fact, product teams, and the services they create, are perhaps the largest and most important data consumers in your organization.

These services do not exist in isolation. They all take some data as input, perform some process or take some action, and return new data as output. And when it comes to input data, they have the same expectations as any other data consumer. They need to understand what data is available, how it is structured, and any other context around the data. They need to know how dependable, correct, and available that data is. They need to know where that data comes from, who owns it, and the support levels being provided.

Often, these services make data available synchronously to each other through HTTP-based APIs, and it's those APIs that define the expectations. The APIs also provide the interface over which this data can be accessed. This is illustrated in the following diagram:

Figure 4.3 – Synchronous inter-service communication, direct between services

However, it's becoming increasingly common to move data asynchronously between services by adopting patterns such as microservices or event-driven architectures, and using a message broker such as Apache Kafka and Google Cloud Pub/Sub, as illustrated in the following diagram:

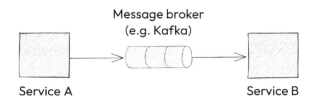

Figure 4.4 – Asynchronous inter-service communication, with a message broker

These are tools and patterns that also have widespread usage in data platforms and are used to provide data to data engineering teams and other data practitioners.

This is why data contracts are often referred to as an API for data. If we think about them from a software architecture point of view, they both provide interfaces between generators and consumers, with the same goals around dependability and the setting of expectations.

We've found that data contracts add a lot of benefits to these architecture patterns, irrespective of whether that same data is also made available for use by data practitioners. In fact, at the time of writing, nearly 80% of the asynchronous communication between services at GoCardless uses data contracts to define these interfaces, and that's growing every month as we continue to adopt data contracts.

In addition, by using the same concepts and tooling around our data, no matter who creates or consumes it, we open up data that had previously been generated solely for data teams to the rest of the organization. That's because it doesn't really matter who generates it or how. What matters are the expectations that have been set around that data, and whether they satisfy the requirements of the consumers.

This opens our existing data to many more use cases. You can use this data to build products and drive services that are more critical to a business, and you can do so with confidence because you know what to expect.

As these products are driven by your data, they can differentiate your business from your competitors and greatly increase your defensibility. No one else has the data you have, and the more you can leverage it, the better the business outcomes. It becomes an *asset*, with real economic value for your organization.

You can then monitor the use of these assets and the business processes they are associated with, using this as a measure of the business value generated through your data, proving the return on your investment in your data products.

Of course, all the while, your organization evolves, and your data needs to too. Therefore, you need a way to support that evolution without impacting these products and services. In the next section, we'll look at how to manage that evolution with data contracts.

Managing the evolution of data

Data evolves over time, just as your organization does, and we'll need to manage that appropriately in order to minimize the impact of that evolution on downstream users – particularly the most critical use cases. However, just like your organization, your core models and data products will also be stable over many years.

You can see that reflected in the public APIs, for those that have them, and how little they change over time. There's little reason why our internal data products should change much more frequently than those if we build them with the same discipline and a product mindset.

Given that, it's fine for there to be some friction when it comes to evolving our data contracts. In fact, this friction is *desirable*. By having some friction here, we're signifying the importance of the data contract and the commitment we make to its maintenance and stability over the long term.

How much friction there should be depends on the type of change we make to the contract, and whether it is a breaking or non-breaking change.

A non-breaking change has no effect on those that already consume the data if they consume it as documented. An example would be adding a new field to a contract. Consumers should just ignore that field, and no code changes or changes to a dashboard would be required.

A breaking change would require data consumers to make changes to their services, or their analytics to be compatible with the change. It could be that a field has been removed and they need to get that data from somewhere else, or it could be a larger refactor of the data due to changing business requirements.

For a non-breaking change, there is little reason to introduce much friction. You want the change to be considered and made for a reason, but it should not affect the stability or dependability of the data.

However, for a breaking change, there *should* be friction. We don't want to release these changes without considering the impact on downstream consumers. They need to be notified ahead of time so that they can give their feedback on the changes, ensuring that they don't impact their use of the data. They then need time to make the required changes to their applications, avoiding any unplanned downtime.

There should be a documented migration path to manage this transition. In many cases, that may require both data contracts to be populated alongside each other for a certain period to ease the migration to the new version.

In larger organizations, it can be difficult to get visibility on all downstream consumers accessing a dataset and how they use it. Data lineage tools can be used to provide this information, which can be used to plan the migration and determine when it is safe to remove a previous version of a data contract. We'll cover data lineage in more detail in *Chapter 9, Implementing Data Contracts in Your Organization*, in the *Discovering data contracts* section.

Of course, how much you invest in this migration depends on the importance of this dataset and the expectations you have set up front. If you have set the expectation that this dataset comes with low or no support, has no SLOs, and so on, and your consumers have accepted that, then maybe you don't need to spend so much time on the migration when you evolve your data.

In this case, you're favoring your agility over providing stability for your consumers. Personally, I'd question the usefulness of any data that has such low expectations, and whether anyone would want to build anything of any value on top of that data if it could change at any time and its correctness is not guaranteed.

All in all, the main thing is ensuring that the *expectations are clear* and have been defined in a data contract.

Summary

In this chapter, we clearly defined the different roles of the data consumer and the data generator, as well as what each expects from the other. We also went into detail on the responsibilities and accountabilities of each role. It's by defining these roles and responsibilities that we enable these groups of people to work together closely and effectively, with the knowledge of what is expected of them.

We use data contracts to provide a clear understanding of responsibility and ownership for each of those roles. And it's by bringing these roles closer together that we improve the accessibility and quality of our data, along with the business value we can generate from it.

Data generators need to feel a sense of ownership over those outcomes if they are to be incentivized to provide data that consumers can build on with confidence. They get that from data consumers, who can share what they need and why they need it.

These consumers include the product teams. In fact, they could be the most important consumers in an organization. We discussed how, by feeding data back to the product teams with well-defined expectations, we can unlock a whole host of different use cases. We can use this data as an asset, powering data-driven products that differentiate our business from our competitors and build defensibility.

Finally, we considered how data evolves over time, just like our organization. However, like the organization, there is a lot of stability in our data, so it's fine if there is some friction when data evolves. In fact, it is *desirable*. We can't confidently build on data that changes all the time, and the friction is relative to the importance of stable, quality data.

However, there is more to be done if we are to achieve this goal. If our data has value and is to be an asset, it's critical that we have the right governance in place to manage it over the long term, and we need to ensure that we are compliant with our data policies and external regulations. We'll explore this in detail in the next chapter as we look at how we can embed data governance into our data contracts.

Further reading

For more information on the topics covered in this chapter, please see the following resources:

- *Roles and responsibilities: Why defining them is important* by Kay Rose: `https://www.betterup.com/blog/roles-and-responsibilities-why-define-them`

- *Eliminating the Data Creation Tax* by Imran Patel: `https://www.syftdata.com/blog/eliminating-the-data-creation-tax`

- *Data as an Asset: Realizing the Economic Potential of Data*: `https://atlan.com/data-as-an-asset/`

- *The Golden Rule of Value* by Joe Reis: `https://joereis.substack.com/p/the-golden-rule-of-value`

- *Designing Event-Driven Systems*: `https://www.confluent.io/resources/ebook/designing-event-driven-systems/`

- Kleppmann, M. (2016). *Designing Data-Intensive Applications*. O'Reilly

- Dean, A. and Crettaz, V. (2019). *Event Streams in Action*. Manning

- *How we evolve APIs* by Robert Fink: `https://blog.palantir.com/how-we-evolve-apis-60dbcfecc439`

- *Tips for successful API migration* by Pooja Nihalani: `https://www.linkedin.com/pulse/tips-successful-api-migration-pooja-nihalani/`

5

Embedding Data Governance

In this chapter, we're going to look at the rather broad area of data governance. We'll explore what we mean by data governance, and why it's so important.

As we'll see, effective governance of data is critical to an organization, but rarely achieved. With data contracts, we can embed our data governance controls alongside the data. We'll show you how to do this and how *powerful* it can be, as it unlocks an array of potential automation and tooling that makes it easy to manage our data.

Finally, we'll assign responsibility for data governance. As we learned in the previous chapter, it's by clearly defining roles and responsibilities that we enable groups of people to work together closely and do so effectively with the knowledge of what is expected of them.

These roles and responsibilities look different in a data contract-backed architecture than in more traditional implementations of data governance, but as we'll discuss, they strike a much better balance between promoting agility and speed of data use and the management of risk.

In this chapter, we're going to cover the following main topics:

- Why we need data governance
- Promoting data governance through data contracts
- Assigning responsibility for data governance

Why we need data governance

We'll start by discussing what we mean by **data governance**, what it covers, and why it is needed. Once we have a shared understanding, we'll look at how we can promote effective data governance through data contracts, and finish by discussing the roles and responsibilities involved.

There are many definitions of data governance, and organizations implement it in different ways. Broadly, it is a combination of *people, processes, standards,* and *technology* that supports and promotes data that is *accessible, usable, accurate, consistent, secure,* and *compliant*.

The following diagram illustrates the data requirements supported by data governance using a combination of different programs:

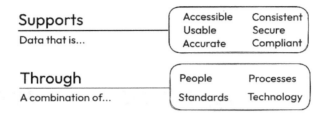

Figure 5.1 – Data requirements supported by the different data governance programs

To gain a better understanding of what data governance is and why we need it, let's explore the following topics in more detail:

- The requirements of data governance
- How data governance programs are typically applied

The requirements of data governance

Ensuring our data is secure and compliant is one of the primary goals of data governance.

There are two types of data when it comes to law. There is *personal data*, where the handling and transformation of that data are governed by increasingly strict rules. And then there is *non-personal data*, which is mostly unregulated.

> **Personal data versus Personally Identifiable Information (PII)**
>
> The terms personal data and **PII** are often used interchangeably, but legally are not the same. Personal data refers to *any* information that relates to an individual, such as their name, address, photographs, and so on. PII is a subset of personal data that specifically refers to information that can be used to identify someone, for example, their social security number, financial account information, and biometric data.
>
> This distinction is important when it comes to understanding what data is affected by different regulations. For example, the **General Data Protection Regulation** (**GDPR**) in the European Union regulates the handling of *personal data*, that is, the broader definition.

When it comes to personal data, an increasing number of regulations passed in countries and territories around the world demand that the data is managed responsibly and kept accurate, complete, and true. More specifically, there may be legal obligations that require organizations to track the following information about the data:

- How they obtained this data.

- The purpose of processing. This includes why they are handling the data and whether it is involved in any decisions – including decisions made by ML models.

- Whether the data has undergone any transformation, such as anonymization or pseudonymization.

- The retention period for this data, and the legal reasons why we must keep the data for that period.

- Whether the data can be accessed and attributed to a specific person.

- Whether the use of the data is ethical, and in line with the values of the organization.

- The physical location of the data and where it might be used.

- Risk assessments for certain activities.

These legal obligations are becoming stricter, and the penalties for violation greater. Therefore, it is increasingly important to handle personal data appropriately and to be able to demonstrate your compliance.

Moreover, the size of data continues to grow dramatically and includes ever more sensitive data. The use cases for that data are also growing, as is the number of people who need access to the data. That's something we want to encourage! But also, something that increases the risks.

Due to several high-profile stories on data misuse and data leaks in recent years, regulators across the world are passing laws to ensure data is managed to a certain standard. They are also under pressure from an increasingly skeptical public, concerned about the misuse of their personal data.

For example, the **European Union (EU)** is currently working on an **artificial intelligence (AI)** Act, which aims to strictly govern data specifically used in AI applications. It proposes a risk-based approach, ranking risks from minimal to unacceptable, with the riskiest applications required to take on more accountability and provide greater transparency of those AI applications expected behavior and the data they use.

While it will only apply to organizations operating in the EU, the act will likely have a global impact, as other countries and territories start drafting their own regulations with increased urgency following the release of ChatGPT and other recent advancements in AI applications.

This is just one example of an upcoming regulation that affects the handling and use of data, but there is a clear direction of travel towards greater regulation of technology in general, and data specifically. Organizations need to start preparing for this *now*, by establishing effective governance structures that meet the requirements today and are flexible enough to meet any future requirements. The failure to prepare could be costly, and organizations found to have mishandled or misused data could suffer large fines and damage to their brands and reputations that may be difficult to recover from.

Now we've understood the key requirements for data governance, let's see how data governance programs designed to meet those requirements are typically applied today.

How data governance programs are typically applied

Data governance teams define policies and standards to support the handling of data in accordance with the regulatory requirements they operate under. They may also provide tooling to help track this information and ensure it is kept up to date. This allows an organization to prove it has met its regulatory requirements and pass any related audits.

Often this is a very manual process, with a centralized team trying to keep an inventory or catalog up to date. Therefore, few organizations can claim to have an accurate, complete, or true inventory of everything they do with the personal data they collect.

More successful data governance initiatives can also be used to promote the *data culture* of the organization. They take the lead in educational initiatives to promote data literacy, which improves the accessibility of the data. They also set standards for the effective use of data across the business, showing how data can be used to drive decisions.

This could be accelerated by defining and building better processes for collaboration between data generators and consumers. There could also be the creation of roles within the business to allocate responsibility for stewarding and championing data.

Unfortunately, data governance has a bit of a bad reputation today. The way it's been implemented in organizations means it is often seen as a central gatekeeper on how data can be used, with a committee reviewing that use. That committee is primarily concerned with reducing risk, and therefore is incentivized to slow down or block the use of data – particularly in areas they are less familiar with.

This leads to one of two outcomes. You could let this become a bottleneck that limits the amount of data that's available to use and get value from, just like the data engineering bottlenecks we discussed in *Chapter 1, A Brief History of Data Platforms*.

Or you can choose to only apply governance to a select few of your critical datasets. The rest will not be managed in accordance with your policies and standards. They become unusable, lose their accuracy, and become inconsistent. If they contain personal data, they will not be managed securely and become non-compliant. They increase your overall risk of data misuse and data leaks.

With data contracts, we will promote a different way of implementing data governance. We'll empower decisions to be made by those closest to the data and give them the autonomy to do so. We'll support them with the right guidance and tooling, supplied by the experts and available to everyone.

Let's explore how data contracts can promote effective data governance in the next section.

Promoting data governance through data contracts

Data contracts are the perfect place to promote data governance. In this section, we'll explore how you can use data contracts to improve the visibility of data governance, collect up-to-date categorization of data, and provide the tooling and guardrails the data generators need to handle their data effectively.

As mentioned in *Chapter 2, Introducing Data Contracts*, the contract definition can be extended to capture any metadata we need to ensure we're handling our data in accordance with our standards. This could include the following:

- Whether it is personal data.

- What entity the data relates to (for example, is it about a customer, an order, or another entity?).

- Who has access to the data, and when that access expires.

- How the data is classified according to your organization's policies (for example, is it confidential, secret, or public knowledge?).

- How long we keep this data for (the retention period).

- The deletion or anonymization policy to apply when the data needs to be removed.

- The physical location of the data.

Having this metadata defined *with* the data ensures it is accurate and complete, and kept up to date as the data evolves.

We're intentionally being very explicit about how we populate the metadata around the data and asking this to be done by the owner of the data contract. It's the only way we can build an accurate, complete, and true inventory of our data assets and how we use them.

Having the task of completing this metadata become a daily activity also increases the visibility of data governance and the risks associated with handling data. Just like any other management of risk, such as securing services or managing passwords, handling data correctly is something everyone should understand and have some accountability for.

This metadata, and the rest of the data contract, is machine readable. We can use it to implement validation and guardrails on the contract to ensure the metadata is being set correctly, alerting the author to any issues. It also enables us to build tooling that supports the correct handling of the data by data generators.

For example, we can use the classifications of the data to automate the access rights for that data. You could grant people holding certain roles in your organization permission to access confidential data for customers that reside in their physical location, based on how the data has been classified. As the data evolves and new data contracts are created, that permission is automatically applied and kept in sync.

By implementing access controls through data contracts and the change management processes we have in place for them, we're increasing the autonomy of data generators and consumers and improving the accessibility of our data. With the right guardrails and guidelines, we empower decisions on access to data to be made locally, while managing the risk at an acceptable level.

Another example would be to automate the deletion and anonymization process. When the data has passed its retention period, or if an individual asks for their personal data to be removed, a service could use the policies defined within the data contract to carry out that task. As the owner of the contract, the data generator doesn't need to know everything about these processes or become an expert in data regulations. They just need to categorize their data in line with how they use it. We demonstrate how to implement this tooling in *Chapter 8, A Sample Implementation*, in the *Implementing contract-driven tooling* section.

Furthermore, we could bring all this metadata, and the actions taken on the data, into a central privacy tool that catalogs the use of data across the organization. From there, it can be regularly reviewed internally and by external auditors.

That's just a few examples, but there are many more use cases and process automations that are enabled by having a complete and accurate set of metadata defined in the data contract. As illustrated in the following diagram, the metadata is the source of truth, and can be presented from the data contract and used wherever it needs to be, depending on how your organization manages the data:

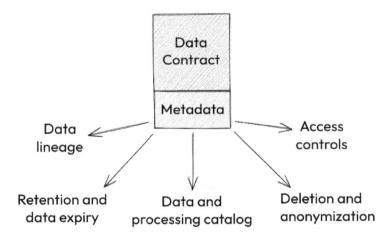

Figure 5.2 – Data governance tooling driven by data contract metadata

We'll be looking further at how we can build tooling and automation driven by data contracts in *Chapter 7, A Contract-Driven Data Architecture*.

In the meantime, let's explore the roles and responsibilities for data governance when building on data contracts.

Assigning responsibility for data governance

To implement effective data governance in our organization, we need to be clear on the roles and responsibilities involved. In this section, we'll define those roles and responsibilities and how they work together.

We will cover this in the following subsections:

- Responsibilities of the data generators
- Introducing a data architecture council
- Working together to implement federated data governance

Responsibilities of the data generators

By using a data contracts-backed architecture, we promote a more decentralized operating model. We give data generators the autonomy and responsibility to own and manage their data, supported by the right self-served tooling and guardrails.

Consequently, we need to rethink our approach to data governance. We don't want to create a central team to try to take control of the data. These teams become a *bottleneck*, slowing down access to and use of data. They also don't have the full context of the data, what it contains, and why we are generating it. Nor can they directly change or improve how the data is generated.

The only people that do have that context and ability are the data generators. Therefore, they must ultimately take responsibility for the governance of that data. That's not as much work as it might sound! With data contracts, the data generators are largely responsible for populating the metadata that describes the data in the contract and keeping it up to date. This would include whether the data is personal or not, classifying the data based on its sensitivity, and defining the deletion or anonymization policies. The rest is automated away through tooling.

We'll cover exactly how they can define this metadata when we look at creating a data contract in *Chapter 6, What Makes Up a Data Contract*, but the following snippet shows an example YAML-based data contract with two fields, name and email, categorized as containing personal data and with an anonymization strategy defined:

```
fields:
  name:
    type: string
    description: The name of the customer.
    personal_data: true
    anonymization_strategy: hex
  email:
    type: string
    description: The email address of the customer.
```

```
personal_data: true
anonymization_strategy: email
```

That should be all a data generator needs to do! They are then supported in making the decisions on how to categorize the data and how to manage that data through a combination of people, processes, standards, and technology. For example, the standards should define the different classifications in use in the organization. Technology can ensure they are applied correctly, such as ensuring all personal data has a specified anonymization policy.

This support can be provided in part through a data governance council. We'll explore this council and its responsibilities in the next subsection.

Introducing the data architecture council

One of the ways we can bring together the different people required to support data governance is to introduce a *data governance council*. This is a central, cross-functional group of people representing different parts of the business who pool their expertise. Together, they have the responsibility to define the data governance policies and standards and identify areas where tooling can be introduced to support the correct implementation of these policies and standards.

In this section, we'll introduce a data governance council and the roles involved before providing some guidance on how to set one up. We'll cover the following topics:

- The roles on the data governance council
- Setting up a data governance council

The roles on the data governance council

Data governance councils come in many different shapes and sizes, and exactly what it should look like depends on your organization and your governance requirements. However, there are certain roles that should be present and certain responsibilities they should be accountable for if they are to be successful.

The council should have representatives from each area of the business that generates or consumes data. This could be the data product manager for that area, or someone else from that business area who is taking on that role. They are responsible for the *quality* and *fit* of the data products they own. They bring to the council any concerns about their ability to deliver those data products.

The council should also have some of your organization's legal, privacy, and security experts. These are the people who know the most about the regulations you need to comply with in the different parts of the world in which you operate. They bring to the council the data-handling requirements and can also clarify the internal classifications and policies.

Finally, there are the representatives of the team implementing data contracts and the tooling it drives. Typically, this is the product manager and/or tech lead of the data platform or data infrastructure team.

They are responsible for implementing and deploying the technology based on the requirements that come out of council discussions. We discuss this tooling and make the case for a data infrastructure team in *Chapter 7, A Contract-Driven Data Architecture.*

There may be other roles represented. For example, you may have people representing the key data stakeholders, such as BI analysts or data scientists. You may also appoint someone with a strong managerial background to lead the council and run it effectively.

With these roles in mind, let's now discuss how to set up a data governance council in your organization.

Setting up a data governance council

As we mentioned in the previous section, exactly what the data governance council should look like depends on your organization and your data governance requirements. So, the first step towards setting up a data governance council is to be clear on the scope and objectives of the council. As we've discussed throughout this chapter, this might include bringing together different roles within the organization, defining or refining policies and standards to make them easier to follow and implement, and promoting a data-driven culture through education and other activities.

Once you're clear on your objectives you can start to consider the people you need on the council and their roles. You'll want to have a balance of technical expertise, business representation, and governance oversight, whilst also ensuring that everyone on that council is going to be an active participant in achieving these objectives. The membership should be limited to no more than 10 participants at a time, as the more people you have on the council, the harder it will be to have effective conversations and make decisions.

You may also need to secure sponsorship of the council from a senior leader or one of your executives. This helps give some authority to the council and assigns accountability for its success to both the sponsor and the members. This accountability also encourages members to prioritize their contribution to the council and its deliveries.

The sponsor could be the leader or chair of the council but doesn't have to be. However, someone needs to be assigned this role and will be the one facilitating the discussions and the other activities carried out by the council, ensuring the focus remains on meeting the objectives you defined.

The council, its membership, and its objectives should be visible to the rest of the organization. You should favor transparency and regularly communicate your discussions and activities and how they contribute towards meeting your objective.

You should now have everything in place to get started! The leader of the council can then organize the meetings and bring these key people together to support your data generators and improve your organization's data governance.

Now we've defined the responsibilities of the data generators and introduced how a data governance council can support them, let's see how they work together to implement an effective model of data governance.

Working together to implement federated data governance

As we discussed, the data governance council is responsible for defining the policies and standards and keeping them up to date. This includes providing a single definition for the terms used to classify data, and the processes to follow when granting access to that data.

However, the council must also ensure these policies strike the right balance between managing the risks and promoting agility in the use of data to drive business value.

One way to achieve this is to explicitly give data generators the autonomy to make decisions locally about how to classify their data. There should be adequate standards and documentation to help that decision, defined by the central data governance council. There could also be guardrails implemented in the technology layer to protect against common mistakes.

But despite that, we must acknowledge that these data generators are human, and are not experts in privacy regulation. They will make mistakes. But for most organizations, this provides a good trade-off between allowing teams to move fast and managing the risk to an acceptable level. It avoids putting in a bottleneck, where any generation of data requires a review from a central team before it can be made available, in the unobtainable pursuit of reducing risk to zero.

We can apply this model of responsibility to any of the data governance activities we explored at the start of this chapter. What that gives us is a central council that brings together the right people to define the processes and standards and supply the right self-served tools to implement them. Together this enables data generators to locally manage data that is accessible, usable, accurate, consistent, secure, and compliant.

The following diagram shows the different data requirements supported by data governance programs, as we had in *Figure 5.1*, but this time showing the responsibilities:

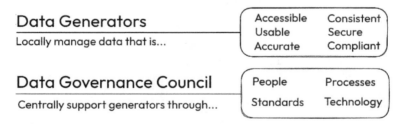

Figure 5.3 – Responsibilities of data governance

This is sometimes described as *federated data governance*. It's also one of the principles of data mesh, as we covered in *Chapter 2, Introducing Data Contracts*. By using data contracts, we can safely promote autonomy and local decision making. With the support of a central data governance council, we can strike the right balance between moving fast and managing our risk.

Summary

In this chapter, we looked at what data governance is and discussed why the effective governance of data is critical. This is particularly important when we look at how we handle our data and manage the risks associated with that. But data governance is more than managing risk, and when done well can help promote a data-driven culture in your organization.

We then looked at how, with data contracts, we can embed our data governance alongside the data. This ensures the classifications and other metadata are correct, accurate, and kept up to date as the data evolves. That metadata can also be used to drive tooling and services to support the effective management and handling of our data, ideally by automating a lot of it away.

With that in place, we're able to assign the responsibility of data governance to the data generators. They are the best placed to carry out that task, as only they have the full context of the data, what it contains, and why we are generating it. They are supported in this task by the data governance council, which brings together the people needed to define the policies and standards used to manage our data and build the technology to support those policies.

This gives us a model of *federated data governance*, where decisions are made locally by data generators, supported by the central data governance council. It strikes the right balance between the management of risk and promoting agility in our use of data to drive business value.

In the next chapter, we'll start looking at how to implement data contracts, starting with what exactly makes up a data contract.

Further reading

For more information on the topics covered in this chapter, please see the following resources:

- Madsen, L. (2019). *Disrupting Data Governance: A Call to Action*. Technics Publications

- Eryurek, E. Gilad, U. Lakshmanan, V. Kibunguchy-Grant, A. Ashdown, J. (2021). *Data Governance: The Definitive Guide*. O'Reilly Media, Inc.

- *The European Union's draft Artificial Intelligence Act*: `https://eur-lex.europa.eu/legal-content/EN/TXT/HTML/?uri=CELEX:52021PC0206&from=EN`

- *How Europe is leading the world in building guardrails around AI* by Kelvin Chan: `https://apnews.com/article/tech-ai-artificial-intelligence-europe-eu-15ac394679519084478e15217c156abc`

- *Tide's Story of GDPR Compliance: Embedding Privacy into Automated Processes*: `https://humansofdata.atlan.com/2023/02/tide-gdpr-automated-privacy/`

- *Data Governance, but Make It a Team Sport* by Maggie Hays: `https://towardsdatascience.com/data-governance-but-make-it-a-team-sport-30dc0164fb7c`

- *Data Governance Has a Serious Branding Problem* by Prukalpa Sankar: `https://humansofdata.atlan.com/2021/11/data-governance-branding-problem/`

- *Data Governance Checklist* by the U.S. Department of Education: `https://nces.ed.gov/Forum/pdf/data_governance_checklist.pdf`

- Dehghani, Z. (2022). *Data Mesh*. O'Reilly Media, Inc.

- *Data governance council - what is it and why do you need one?* By George Firican: `https://www.lightsondata.com/data-governance-council/`

- *Data Mesh 101: Why Federated Data Governance Is the Secret Sauce of Data Innovation* by Seb Bulpin: `https://www.mesh-ai.com/blog-posts/data-mesh-101-federated-data-governance`

- *How to Create a Data Governance Team? 3 Essential Steps* by Tanmay Sarkar: `https://www.moderndatastack.xyz/journal/how-to-create-a-data-governance-team-3-essential-steps-4e01`

Part 3: Designing and Implementing a Data Architecture Based on Data Contracts

In this part, we'll look at exactly how to design and implement data contracts, including a sample implementation, and provide practical advice to implement data contracts in your organization.

This part comprises the following chapters:

- *Chapter 6, What Makes Up a Data Contract*
- *Chapter 7, A Contract-Driven Data Architecture*
- *Chapter 8, A Sample Implementation*
- *Chapter 9, Implementing Data Contracts in Your Organization*
- *Chapter 10, Data Contracts in Practice*

What Makes Up a Data Contract

In this chapter, we're going to look at what exactly makes up a data contract. This includes the **schema**, which describes and documents the structure of the data. We'll discuss why this is important and show how we can define the schema in several open source schema formats.

A schema can only describe data at a point in time. However, as the needs of the organization change, so too does our data. We'll explore how we can support the evolution of our data, while still providing data consumers the stability they need to build on this data with confidence.

However, data contracts are *more* than just a schema. As we've discussed in previous chapters, we need our data contracts to capture metadata that describes how the data can be used, how it is governed, and the controls around the data. We'll show how we do that, and how we can use that metadata to drive tooling and integrate with other services.

By the end of this chapter, we'll have seen how the makeup of a data contract unlocks a whole range of possibilities, which, along with the culture change we've discussed previously, enables an organization to get the most value from its data.

In this chapter, we're going to cover the following main topics:

- The schema of a data contract
- Evolving your data over time
- Defining governance and controls

The schema of a data contract

We'll start this section by looking at the schema of a data contract, what to put in it, and why. Then we'll look at how to make these schemas accessible to both data generators and consumers, by storing them in a system (or a *registry*) that is recognized as the source of truth.

We'll cover these topics in the following subsections:

- Defining a schema
- Using a schema registry as the source of truth

Defining a schema

The schema defines the *structure* of the data. At a minimum, it will hold the complete list of the fields available and their data type.

The following code block shows an example of a schema that defines a `Customer` record with fields and their types using Protocol Buffers (`https://protobuf.dev`), as well as a unique field number, as required by Protocol Buffers:

```
message Customer {
    string id       = 1;
    string name     = 2;
    string email    = 3;
    string language = 4;
}
```

All data contracts *must* have a schema that defines the structure of the data.

Data that is well structured is easier for a data consumer to consume. It sets some basic expectations around the data, what will be present, and how it is presented. It is the minimum bar in guaranteeing the *quality* of the data.

Schemas can also be used by tooling to further increase the ease of use. For example, if using an open standard, there will almost certainly be open source libraries that help with efficiently encoding and decoding the data backed by the schema.

Some services are also able to ingest these schemas and use that to drive some functionality. Examples include data catalogs, data governance tools, and data validation services.

Many schema formats can hold more than just the list of fields and their types. For example, when using Apache Avro (`https://avro.apache.org`) we can add some documentation to the schema to help the consumer understand the context of that field.

The following code block shows a schema in Apache Avro holding the same `Customer` record we saw earlier in Protocol Buffers, with the added documentation highlighted:

```
{
    "type": "record",
    "name": "Customer",
    "doc": "A customer of our e-commerce website",
    "fields": [
```

```
{
  "name": "id",
  "type": "string",
  "doc": "The unique identifier for the customer."
},
{
  "name": "name",
  "type": "string",
  "doc": "The name of the customer."
},
{
  "name": "email",
  "type": "string",
  "doc": "The email address of the customer."
},
{
  "name": "language",
  "type": "string",
  "doc": "The language preference of the customer."
}
  ]
}
```

Both Apache Avro and Protocol Buffers are *serialization frameworks*. They use their schemas to encode the data in a compact binary format that can be efficiently serialized and deserialized. There are other open source schema formats that have different aims, including JSON Schema (https://json-schema.org), which simply uses JSON for serialization but has other features, including the validation of data.

The following code block is an example of JSON Schema holding the same Customer record we've seen in Apache Avro and Protocol Buffers. The parts that define the data validations are highlighted:

```
{
  "$schema": "http://json-schema.org/draft-07/schema#",
  "type": "object",
  "title": "customer",
  "description": "A customer of our e-commerce website",
  "properties": {
    "id": {
      "type": "string",
      "description": "The unique identifier for the customer.",
    },
    "name": {
      "type": "string",
```

```
      "description": "The name of the customer.",
    },
    "email": {
      "type": "string",
      "description": "The email address of the customer.",
      "pattern": "^[a-zA-Z0-9._%+-]+@[a-zA-Z0-9.-]+\\.[a-zA-Z]{2,}$"
    },
    "language": {
      "type": "string",
      "description": "The language preference of the customer.",
      "enum": ["en", "fr", "es"]
    }
  },
  "required": ["id", "name", "email", "language"]
}
```

These validations can be used by libraries to prevent incorrect data from being emitted from the source systems. If the data fails validation, an exception will be raised in that service and an alert will be sent to the data generator. They can then resolve the issue before that incorrect data gets to each of their data consumers, reducing the impact caused. We discuss data validations with data contracts in more detail in *Chapter 10, Data Contracts in Practice* , in the *Monitoring and enforcing data contracts* section.

While these schema formats work well for their primary use case of aiding the serialization of data between services, they are not easy to extend to meet different or more advanced use cases, including those we plan to cover with data contracts. That's why most data contract implementations use a higher-level definition language such as YAML (https://yaml.org/) and Jsonnet (https://jsonnet.org/), or even dynamic programming languages such as Python and TypeScript. We discuss why that is in more detail later in this chapter, in the *Defining governance and controls* section, but to round off this discussion, the following shows our JSON Schema converted into YAML:

```
name: Customer
description: A customer of our e-commerce website.
fields:
  id:
    type: string
    description: The unique identifier for the customer.
    required: true
  name:
    type: string
    description: The name of the customer.
    required: true
  email:
    type: string
    description: The email address of the customer.
```

```
      pattern: "^[a-zA-Z0-9._%+-]+@[a-zA-Z0-9.-]+\\.[a-zA-Z]{2,}$"
      required: true
   language:
      type: string
      description: The language preference of the customer.
      enum: [en, fr, es]
```

Now we have implemented the schemas, we need somewhere to store them. This will be the *source of truth* for the schemas we have defined, and accessible to both the data generators and the consumers, and their services. This is known as a **schema registry**, which we'll look at next.

Using a schema registry as the source of truth

The schemas we've implemented can be used by both data generators and data consumers in several different applications.

Both Apache Avro and Protocol Buffers schemas can be used to generate source code. As binary formats, this code must be used by the data generators to write data that conforms to the schema and is serialized correctly. The data consumers also need to use the generated code to deserialize the binary representation into something their code can understand.

While JSON Schema events are serialized in the widely used and text-based JSON format, the schemas can be loaded by libraries to help write the data in the correct format and to run the validation checks.

These schemas can also be used in **Continuous Integration** (**CI**) checks, giving both the generators and consumers confidence that their code is using the data models correctly as they develop their services.

Furthermore, as open formats, these schemas can often be ingested into other applications or used to define resources such as a table in a data warehouse. We discuss these use cases in more detail later in this chapter, in the *Defining governance and controls* section.

When using the schemas across many different applications, we need to ensure they are kept in sync. So, when one application refers to *version 1* of our `Customer` schema, that needs to be the same schema as the next application that refers to it.

We achieve this by creating a central service to store these schemas. This makes the schemas accessible to any application that needs them and acts as our *source of truth* for those schemas. We call this the **schema registry**.

Depending on our requirements, the schema registry can be as simple as a Git repository or a shared folder on a distributed filesystem such as Amazon S3, or a service that presents a rich API for the saving and retrieving of schemas and performing compatibility checks. Whatever we choose to use as our registry, it should be capable of the following:

- Publishing a new schema

- Publishing an updated version of an existing schema

- Retrieving a schema with a particular version, including those superseded by a newer version

- Retrieving the latest version of a schema

There are many schema registry services available, some of which are open source, and some are implemented by platform and cloud providers. Examples include the following:

- *Confluent Schema Registry* (`https://github.com/confluentinc/schema-registry`), which is part of Confluent's Kafka-based platform and supports Apache Avro, JSON Schema, and Protocol Buffers schemas

- *Iglu* (`https://github.com/snowplow/iglu`), an open source registry supporting Apache Avro, JSON Schema, and Apache Thrift schemas

- *AWS Glue Schema Registry* (`https://docs.aws.amazon.com/glue/latest/dg/schema-registry.html`), which is part of the cloud platform and supports schemas defined in Apache Avro, JSON Schema, and Protocol Buffers

However, one drawback of using services such as these is that as more and more data generators and consumers make use of them to serialize and deserialize data, they can become a performance bottleneck and a single source of failure in your architecture. So, you'll need to consider how best to mitigate that potential issue when designing your data architecture.

We've seen how we can implement schemas that define the structure of the data and understand why we need them and the benefits we can derive from them.

However, schemas can only define the structure of the data as it is at a particular point in time. Our data will evolve as our organization evolves, and so the schemas must evolve too. We'll look at how to manage that evolution next.

Evolving your data over time

In this section, we'll discuss how we can manage the evolution of our data, and the schemas that define it, while still giving the data consumers the stability they need to build on the data with confidence.

We spoke in detail about how data evolves in an organization and why managing the evolution of data well is important for consumers in *Chapter 4, Bringing Data Consumers and Generators Closer Together*, in the *Managing the evolution of data* section. We also discussed the difference between a breaking change and a non-breaking change, and how for a breaking change we want to deliberately introduce some friction to ensure the migration to that new version is managed to reduce the impact on downstream consumers.

It's this concept of *versions* that allows us to evolve schemas. We use versioning to track and manage the changes to a schema over time. The previous versions of the schema are used to validate whether the new version introduces any breaking changes.

In this section, we'll look at the following topics:

*   Evolving your schemas
*   Migrating your consumers

Evolving your schemas

When evolving a schema, you need to consider the type of change you are making, and how compatible that change is with your previous version.

Both Apache Avro (`https://avro.apache.org/docs/1.11.1/specification/#schema-resolution`) and Protocol Buffers (`https://protobuf.dev/programming-guides/proto3/#updating`) clearly define the rules for schema compatibility in their specifications, but essentially the rules are the same for any schema format.

Based on those rules, the change will either be a **non-breaking** change or a **breaking** change.

Let's walk through these changes using the example Protocol Buffers schema from earlier in this chapter, as follows:

```
message Customer {
    string id       = 1;
    string name     = 2;
    string email    = 3;
    string language = 4;
}
```

A non-breaking schema change means that data generated against a new version of the schema can still be read by a service using any previous version of the schema, without any data loss or other impact. Similarly, data generated against the previous version of the schema can be read by the new version. Examples of a non-breaking change include adding a new optional field and removing a field that is not required and has a default value specified.

Adding a new `address` field to our schema as follows is a non-breaking change:

```
message Customer {
   string id       = 1;
   string name     = 2;
   string email    = 3;
   string language = 4;
   string address  = 5;
}
```

This change has no impact on existing data consumers, as they simply ignore the `address` field. Those who need the added field can upgrade to the latest schema once it's been released and update their code to start using it.

As non-breaking changes are low impact, data generators should be able to make these changes with *low friction*.

A breaking change is anything that does have an impact on existing data consumers. For example, removing a required field would result in data generated against the new schema being invalid to any consumers using the existing schema. Another example would be changing the data type of a field, such as from a string to an integer.

Removing the `email` field from our schema, as shown in the following code snippet, is a breaking change:

```
message Customer {
   string id       = 1;
   string name     = 2;
   string language = 4;
}
```

This change will immediately impact any existing data consumers. It could cause their pipelines and applications to fail or break any dashboards built on this data. Given the impact, we may choose to *add friction* to limit these changes, setting the expectation that they should be relatively infrequent and promoting the stability of the schemas.

These changes can and will still happen, so when making a breaking change, we'll need to create a plan to aid the consumers as they migrate to the new version. Let's talk about migrating data consumers next.

Migrating your consumers

A data generator may need to evolve their data and create a new version of a schema and a data contract for a few reasons. It may be required to meet new requirements from one or more data consumers, or it may be needed to allow the data generator to make changes to their service that support new features or improve its performance.

The first thing a data generator should do is discuss the changes with their data consumers and ensure the new version of the data contract still meets their requirements. Once that has been agreed, they need to consider how they will migrate their consumers to that new version, without causing major disruption or breaking existing applications unexpectedly. They can manage this through the creation of a *migration plan.*

What that migration plan will look like depends on the size of the change, the criticality of the data, and the number of consumers of that data. If the data has one or two consumers and the change is relatively small, you might run the two versions side by side for just a couple of weeks while the consumers upgrade to the newest version. If it's a larger change or affects many consumers, then you might need to produce data for each version for a longer period and consider providing libraries to ease the migration.

The important thing is that there is a plan, and that plan has been agreed between the data generator and their consumers. This aligns strongly with our aims of bringing data generators and consumers together, as we discussed in detail in *Chapter 4, Bringing Data Consumers and Generators Closer Together.*

All of this does *introduce friction* for the data generator and slow them down, but that is deliberate. It's this friction that prevents these changes from happening without consideration. It shows that we are favoring *stability over agility*, which is what we need if we want reliable data consumers can trust and build on with confidence.

The use of schemas, and the support for schema evolution on those schemas, are key to implementing data contracts and using them to increase the dependability and quality of our data. But it's not just the schema we want to manage – it's the data itself, and the way we use it to further the goals of the organization.

To that end, we also want to define the governance and controls around the data and manage that just as effectively as we do the schemas. The next section will explore in detail why we want to do that, and how we'll do it.

Defining the governance and controls

In *Chapter 5, Embedding Data Governance*, we discussed the importance of data governance and how we embed those controls alongside the data. We also spoke about how the responsibility of those controls is assigned to the data generators, supported by a central data governance committee through policies, standards, and tooling.

In this section, we'll look at exactly how we can define the governance and controls in the data contract.

Every data contract must have an owner. This is the data generator, and it is they who take on the responsibilities and accountabilities we discussed in *Chapter 4, Bringing Data Consumers and Generators Closer Together.*

Depending on your requirements, you might want to embed some of the following in your data contract:

- The version number of the contract
- **The service-level agreements (SLAs)**
- How to access the data (for example, is the interface a table in a data warehouse, a topic on a stream-processing platform, and so on)
- The primary key(s)
- What entity the data relates to (for example, whether it is about a product, an order, and so on)
- Semantics (for example, units of measure)
- Whether it is personal data
- How the data is classified according to your organization's policies (for example, whether it is confidential, secret, or public knowledge)
- How long we'll keep this data for (the retention period)
- The deletion or anonymization policy to apply when the data needs to be removed
- The physical location of the data

While some of the schema formats we looked at earlier in this chapter are extensible to a degree, they have all been developed primarily to aid the serialization of data sent between services. None have been designed to capture the variety of extensive metadata about the data the schema applies to.

Therefore, we may choose to use a higher-level definition language that can capture this metadata alongside the data. Examples include YAML (`https://yaml.org/`) and Jsonnet (`https://jsonnet.org/`), but could even be dynamic programming languages such as Python and TypeScript. These are flexible enough to capture what we need, in the format we need it. They also provide a balance between being human-friendly and machine-readable.

Which schema definition language to use to define your data contracts depends on your requirements and what is already in use at your organization. For example, at GoCardless we use Jsonnet, as it is the language of choice for our infrastructure platform, and therefore our engineers are already familiar with it. But there's nothing particularly special about Jsonnet that makes it perfect for defining data contracts, so I wouldn't necessarily recommend it if you don't already use it in your organization.

YAML is probably one of the better choices for implementing data contracts. The following code block is an example data contract for our `Customer` record defined in a custom YAML schema, highlighting some of the extra metadata we can define:

```yaml
name: Customer
description: A customer of our e-commerce website.
owner: product-team@data-contracts.com
version: 2
fields:
  id:
    type: string
    description: The unique identifier for the customer.
    required: true
    primary_key: true
  name:
    type: string
    description: The name of the customer.
    required: true
    personal_data: true
    anonymization_strategy: hex
  email:
    type: string
    description: The email address of the customer.
    pattern: "^[a-zA-Z0-9._%+-]+@[a-zA-Z0-9.-]+\\.[a-zA-Z]{2,}$"
    required: true
    personal_data: true
    anonymization_strategy: email
  language:
    type: string
    description: The language preference of the customer.
    enum: [en, fr, es]
```

This custom schema format is the interface you are providing to define the data contract, primarily for use by data generators but also for data consumers to use to discover and understand the data. But it's also machine-readable, so you can use it to integrate with other systems and tools. For example, at GoCardless we use the contract to drive our data handling tooling, which deletes or anonymizes data when we no longer have a legitimate reason to retain it or in response to a request from a customer.

We can also use a data contract to generate a schema in any other format and benefit from the open ecosystem of that format. At GoCardless, we take our Jsonnet data contract and convert it to a valid Protocol Buffers schema. We then apply that schema to a Google Cloud Pub/Sub topic, which enforces schema validation at the infrastructure layer (https://cloud.google.com/pubsub/docs/schemas).

We also convert the same contract to a Google BigQuery table, which is defined in a custom JSON format (`https://cloud.google.com/bigquery/docs/reference/rest/v2/tables#TableSchema`).

We even convert the contract to a valid JSON Schema. Developers can then use one of the many open source JSON Schema libraries to validate the data in their code, before publishing to Pub/Sub or writing to BigQuery.

The following diagram shows how we convert the data contract into these different formats to power our internal data handling tooling and integrate with other services:

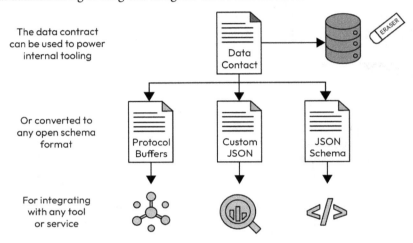

Figure 6.1 – Using the data contract to produce schemas in various formats

In fact, we can convert the data contract into any format we like! This allows us to integrate with any number of tools and services to support data generators, consumers, and other stakeholders. The data contract remains the source of truth for this metadata, with everything else derived from it.

We'll look at further examples of using schemas to drive tooling and automation in *Chapter 7, A Contract-Driven Data Architecture*.

Summary

In this chapter, we've started to see exactly what makes up a data contract. A large part of the data contract is the schema. We explored various open source schema formats to understand how we can use them to define schemas and the different functionality we can add to those schemas. We also looked at how we can make schemas accessible by using a schema registry to act as the source of truth for them.

However, schemas can only define how the data looks at a set point in time. Data will evolve, and so will the schema. So, we then discussed how to evolve your data over time and how to migrate your consumers to a new version without causing major disruption or breaking existing applications unexpectedly.

We finished the chapter by looking at how we can use data contracts to manage the governance and controls of data through the specification of metadata that describes the data.

We can then use that metadata to integrate with any tool or service. This can be done by using the data contract directly, as it is machine-readable, or we can convert the data contract to any number of open and custom schema formats for integration with other services, benefitting from existing ecosystems.

We're going to take this concept further in the next chapter, as we explore how the data contract can be used to create a *contract-driven data architecture*.

Further reading

For more information on the topics covered in this chapter, please see the following resources:

- *Protocol Buffers*: https://protobuf.dev/
- *Apache Avro*: https://avro.apache.org/
- *JSON Schema*: https://json-schema.org/
- *YAML*: https://yaml.org/
- *Jsonnet*: https://jsonnet.org/
- *Schemata*: https://github.com/ananthdurai/schemata
- *Protocol Buffers Best Practices for Backward and Forward Compatibility* by John Gramila: https://earthly.dev/blog/backward-and-forward-compatibility/
- *Understanding Avro Compatibility* by Kyle Carter: https://medium.com/codex/understanding-avro-compatibility-e2f9afa48dd1
- *Understanding JSON Schema Compatibility* by Robert Yokota: https://yokota.blog/2021/03/29/understanding-json-schema-compatibility/
- *Data contracts: The missing foundation* by Tom Baeyens: https://medium.com/@tombaeyens/data-contracts-the-missing-foundation-3c7a98544d2a

- *Template for a data contract used in a data mesh*: `https://github.com/paypal/data-contract-template`

- *Implementing Data Contracts at GoCardless* by Andrew Jones: `https://medium.com/gocardless-tech/implementing-data-contracts-at-gocardless-3b5c49074d13`

7

A Contract-Driven Data Architecture

In the previous chapter, we saw exactly what makes up a data contract. In this chapter, we're going to build on that by looking at how we can use the data contract to drive our data architecture. We'll introduce the concept of a *contract-driven data architecture* and show how powerful this can be. We believe this is a step-change in how we build data platforms, and we'll discuss the many benefits we get when adopting this architecture pattern.

As part of that discussion, we'll introduce the three principles that unlock those benefits: autonomy, guardrails, and consistency, and you'll learn how those principles benefit the data generators, the data consumers, and the organization. To promote autonomy, we need to provide tooling that can be self-served by the data generators. We'll finish this chapter by looking at why that is important and show an example of how to achieve it.

By the end of this chapter, you'll fully understand this new architecture pattern and the benefits of using it, so you can see how you could apply the same ideas in your organization.

In this chapter, we're going to cover the following main topics:

- A step-change in building data platforms
- Introducing the principles of a contract-driven data architecture
- Providing self-served data infrastructure

A step-change in building data platforms

To start this section, we'll explain exactly what we mean by a **contract-driven data architecture**. We'll explore how it is powered by using data contracts as the place to capture the metadata that *describes* the data, and we'll see just how powerful it can be to create a contract-driven data architecture. We'll show why we believe it is a step-change in building data platforms.

We'll finish by walking through a case study from GoCardless, where we implemented a solution we thought was promoting autonomy but wasn't as successful as we expected! What we learned from that greatly influenced our implementation of data contracts, where we have been much more successful in promoting autonomy through a self-serve interface.

We'll explore the following topics in turn:

- Building generic data tooling

- Introducing a data infrastructure team

- A case study from GoCardless in promoting autonomy

- Promoting autonomy through decentralization

Building generic data tooling

Most data engineering teams build tools and services for their own use, to facilitate the movement and preparation of data ready for other data practitioners to consume. These solutions are often tied to a specific use case or deployment.

An example would be a data pipeline that ingests customer data from a third-party service, such as Salesforce, and stores it in the data warehouse. It would be made specifically for that data, writing the data to a specific part of the data warehouse.

There might then be other services that help manage that data, for example, by taking regular backups, or by anonymizing personal data. These services are also written specifically for that data and know exactly how it is structured, with the business logic encoded in the service itself, as part of the code.

A very similar service would then be created for the next third-party service you want to integrate. Then again for a different type of source data, such as a **change data capture** (**CDC**) solution that ingests data from an internal database.

By building point solutions like this, the data engineering team becomes a *bottleneck*. Only they can ingest data into the data warehouse. Only they can manage the data correctly and in accordance with company policies. Each data source becomes a ticket in their backlog, but realistically only the top-priority ones will ever be delivered.

This severely limits the accessibility of data and reduces the value that we can extract from our data.

The following diagram illustrates the duplication when building point solutions to extract data from sources, be they third-party sources such as Salesforce or internal databases using a CDC solution:

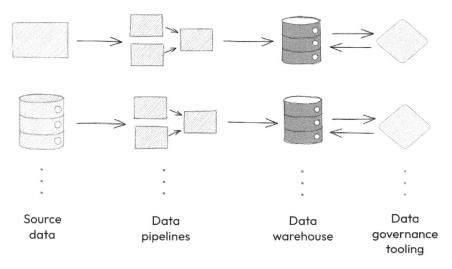

Figure 7.1 – Building data pipelines as point solutions

There's no technical reason why this is the case. Each of the services that make up the pipeline in the earlier example doesn't have to be built for a specific use case or dataset. They just need to know enough *about* the data so they can take the right action. In our example, that would include the following:

- Where in the data warehouse to write the data

- How often to take backups, and how long to keep them for

- The anonymization strategy for each field containing personal data

As we discussed in *Chapter 6, What Makes Up a Data Contract*, we can capture this and other governance- and control-related metadata in the data contract. The following example shows a YAML-based data contract, with the most relevant parts for this discussion highlighted:

```
name: Customer
description: A customer record ingested from Salesforce.
owner: product-team@data-contracts.com
version: 2
warehouse_path: sales_data.salesforce.customers
backups:
  schedule: @daily
  expire: P60D
fields:
  id:
    type: string
    description: The unique identifier for the record.
  name:
```

```
    type: string
    description: The name of the customer.
    personal_data: true
    anonymization_strategy: hex
  email:
    type: string
    description: The email address of the customer.
    personal_data: true
    anonymization_strategy: email
```

With a contract definition like this, in a machine-readable format, we can build the services that made up the pipeline in our example so they can process any data, of any shape, just by using the metadata defined in the data contract.

For example, the service that writes the data to the data warehouse knows the structure of the data from the schema and can use that to ensure the table in the warehouse is present and with the same schema.

Similarly, the backups service can be configured to run daily, as per the cron expression in the contract. It also knows to expire data after 60 days.

And finally, the data handling service can anonymize the personal data when required, as we know how to find the personal data in the data warehouse, and what anonymization strategy to use. In our example, we'll overwrite the customer's name with random hexadecimal characters, and replace the email address with anonymized+<id>@data-contracts.com.

As well as aiding the development of this tooling, defining this metadata as part of the contract increases the visibility of our data handling requirements and makes it clear who is responsible and accountable for the correct handling of the data. We discussed this previously in detail in *Chapter 5, Embedding Data Governance*.

This is obviously a win for the data engineering team. It reduces the effort required to build new pipelines and reduces the number of distinct services they need to maintain. But they are still a bottleneck and still restrict access to data.

We want to remove these bottlenecks wherever we find them. We want to increase the accessibility of data, by empowering data generators to take ownership of the data they create and provide high-quality data products to their data consumers to drive business value.

To enable this, we need to open this tooling – and data contracts – to everyone who generates data. This requires the formation of a team with the focus and remit to build that tooling. We'll discuss this next, and build the case for a *data infrastructure team*.

Introducing a data infrastructure team

To support our data generators – whoever they are – we need to provide them with the tooling that promotes their autonomy and allows them to focus on the data itself. It should be self-serve, with no unnecessary processes adding friction or slowing them down.

For example, we don't need every data generator to be an expert in privacy regulation. We can automate that concern away through the tooling, and by implementing guidelines and guardrails around that tooling. We *do* need the data generators to tell us about the data they are generating, and we *trust* them to do that as best they can. But from then on, the tooling does the right thing.

This tooling and related services should, like all internal tooling (and like our data!) be built and delivered with a product mindset. We treat our customers with empathy. We aim to understand their problems and collaborate with them to provide the right solutions. Those solutions should have a great user experience that *delights* them.

A lot of this is likely to be beyond the remit of the data engineering team, and they may not have the right expertise to do this. Therefore, we'd encourage organizations to set up a dedicated *data infrastructure team* to build and support this tooling.

This team should be made up of software engineers, and possibly **Site Reliability Engineers (SREs)**. They're a central team, best working alongside the other central teams building internal tooling, such as those working on the infrastructure platform and related tooling. The data tooling has a different focus but shouldn't be implemented much differently from the rest of the infrastructure tooling you have. They all have to work well together and provide a seamless experience to both the software and the data engineers.

This is how we are set up at GoCardless, and that helped create the conditions for us to come up with data contracts and implement them so successfully. We're a team of software engineers – not data engineers. We report to the product development function – not the data function. We're focused on enablement through autonomy – not on building a central platform that inevitably becomes a bottleneck.

Of course, we didn't join GoCardless as a data infrastructure team and immediately start working on data contracts! It's been a journey to get here and continues to be a journey as we learn, take feedback, and improve our tooling and our understanding of what we want to build.

There's a step we took on this journey that in hindsight looks like a mistake but is a great case study in our attempts to promote autonomy, without which we may never have created data contracts. Let's walk through that case study now.

A case study from GoCardless in promoting autonomy

As the data infrastructure team at GoCardless, we had always been thinking about how best to promote autonomy to our data generators. In 2018, that led us to implement an application we called the *Data Platform Gateway*.

This was our solution to the proliferation of point solutions we mentioned in the *A step-change in building data platforms* section earlier. It was an application that provided an HTTP-based API, which allowed data generators to push data to the data warehouse. At the time it was the second supported method for getting data into the data warehouse (the first being our change data capture service).

This API validated any events it received against schemas, stored in a schema registry. If the event matched the schema and was valid, it would be sent to a Google Cloud Pub/Sub topic. From there, another service took those events and inserted them into the correct place in the data warehouse, which for us is Google BigQuery.

The schemas themselves were stored and managed in a Git repository, and anyone could add or change a schema without requiring approval from us or any other central team. Once merged into the main branch, the schemas would automatically be pushed to the schema registry and events could then be written.

The overall architecture of the Data Platform Gateway is shown in the following diagram:

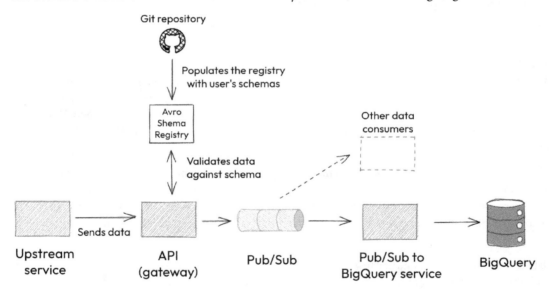

Figure 7.2 – The Data Platform Gateway architecture, showing the key components and services

These schemas themselves were quite basic. They were in a custom YAML format, but that was just a thin abstraction over Apache Avro schemas, which we used under the hood. We didn't have any extra metadata in there beyond the schema.

The following example shows the YAML-based schema we were using:

```
name: transaction_fee_calculated
doc: Records the calculation of a transaction fee that would be
collected from a merchant.
primary_keys:
  - event_id
fields:
  - name: event_id
    doc: Unique deterministic ID of the event.
    type: string
    required: true
  - name: created_at
    doc: RFC 3339 time at which the event was emitted.
    type: timestamp
    required: true
  - name: payment_currency
    doc: >
        ISO 4217 currency code of the payment which this fee is been
charged for.
        Examples include AUD, CAD, DKK, EUR, GBP, NZD, SEK, USD
    type: string
  - name: amount
    doc: The amount (in minor currency unit) of the calculated fee.
    type: long
  - name: net_amount
    doc: The amount (in minor currency unit) of the calculated fee,
minus tax
    type: long
```

The Data Platform Gateway shared some of the same goals we're now realizing with data contracts. We were hoping to promote *autonomy* by allowing teams to specify their own schemas. We also expected teams to consume from the Pub/Sub feed if they needed access to near real-time data or were building event-driven services, which we knew there was some demand for.

Initially, this service was quite successful. The ability to write data directly to the warehouse, from anywhere, was a new capability for us. Several schemas were created by users, who appreciated the autonomy they had to do so without requiring central approval.

However, the use cases were all simple, and the number of schemas created each month soon dropped to single figures and eventually to near zero. We never had anyone consume directly from the Pub/Sub topics.

Meanwhile, other solutions that on the surface were very similar to the Data Platform Gateway were being built in other parts of the organization. We hadn't achieved our goal of removing the need to implement custom point solutions.

So, what went wrong? Let's look at the reasons this wasn't successful, and what we learned.

Promoting autonomy through decentralization

In this section, we'll look at what we learned about why the Data Platform Gateway wasn't a success, and how that influenced the design of data contracts.

After spending some time with the teams to understand why they were spending valuable time building their own solutions instead of using ours, three key concerns with the Data Platform Gateway were highlighted:

- *Disagreement on design choices*: We were opinionated in our design choices, and not everyone shared our opinions! This included choosing Apache Avro as our serialization framework, which had poor support for Ruby – the language of choice for our engineering teams. It also related to the shape of the schemas we supported, which could only be one level deep and only allowed simple data structures.

- *Lack of ownership of the resources and data*: These were still owned and managed by the central data infrastructure team, and any change to them required going through the team. This included granting access to the BigQuery tables and the Pub/Sub topics, and changing the configuration of those resources in order to improve performance. It also included changing the data, for example, to recover from an incident or aid the evolution of a schema (as we discussed in *Chapter 4, Bringing Data Consumers and Generators Closer Together*, in the *Managing the evolution of data* section).

- *Undefined expectations and service-level objectives (SLOs)*: We hadn't set any SLOs on the service, and the data infrastructure team was not on call. This meant users could not depend on it for anything supporting important business processes. Furthermore, a lot of the resources were shared among all users of the Data Platform Gateway, including the API, the schema registry, the Pub/Sub topic, and the service that wrote the data to BigQuery. An issue with any of those would impact everyone's data, even if the issue was localized to a particular dataset or an individual record causing a bug on one of those.

What we'd done was simply move the bottleneck we discussed in *Chapter 1, A Brief History of Data Platforms* – rather than removing it. The Data Infrastructure team became the bottleneck, instead of the Data Engineering team. Furthermore, the data generators were still as far away from the data consumers as before, and there was still a complete lack of collaboration.

The following diagram shows these problems, and as you may notice, it is very similar to *Figure 1.5*:

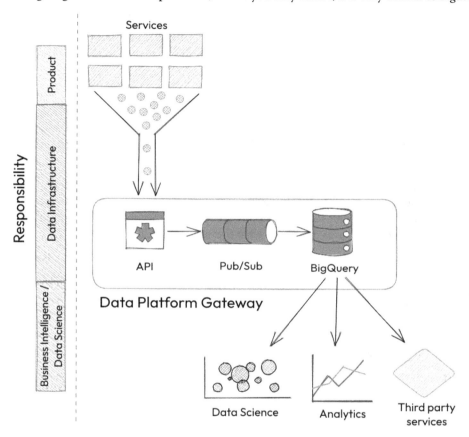

Figure 7.3 – The Data Platform Gateway became a bottleneck, the gap between the data generators and consumers remained, and responsibility did not change

What users were clearly asking for was *more autonomy*. They wanted the autonomy to make some of their own design choices. They wanted the autonomy to manage their resources, and even take on the *responsibility* to do so to ensure those resources and the support around them met the reliability expectations they required.

We took that on board and started thinking about the different ways we could provide our users with as much autonomy as we could, and identified four areas to guide the next iteration of our data platform:

- *Decentralization*: We wanted to design an architecture that allowed them to define their own schemas in their workspace, which would then bring up the required resources in *their* infrastructure, alongside the services they owned.

- *Ownership*: We would explicitly assign them ownership of those resources. This would include granting access, tweaking the configuration, and scaling services up or down depending on the load they were generating. It would also apply to the data within those resources, which they could manage and make changes to as needed. For example, to fix the data following an incident, or to manage the evolution of their schemas.

- *Flexibility*: A more flexible implementation where the data generators had more control over their schemas, the tools they used, and the resources they created would further increase autonomy. We trusted them to provide datasets that met the requirements of their users, without limiting them to follow our opinions on exactly what that should look like.

- *Isolation*: A more decentralized architecture would ensure different datasets are isolated from each other. Each dataset could have its own SLOs and expectations around it, and they would be easier to meet without the worry someone else's data or services could impact your data or services.

Then, considering the schemas themselves, we realized the reason we were so opinionated about them is that it made the development of tooling around that data easier if they were all the same shape.

But it wasn't really the shape we needed to know – it was the *context* of the data. If that context could be defined in metadata alongside the data, and if that metadata was machine-readable, it would only take a little more effort to build the same tooling. In return for that effort, users would have much more flexibility over their data.

And so all this together led us toward creating data contracts and implementing a contract-driven architecture. We believe this is a step-change in how to build data platforms, and having spent the last three years building this, we have proven we are on the right path.

In fact, we have seen teams organically migrate away from their own point solutions and onto data contracts. And that's the best validation we could have had.

The Data Platform Gateway is now decommissioned, with all users moved to data contracts, but it was a key step in our journey toward a contract-driven architecture.

There are many benefits to building data platforms in this way, and while we've mentioned some examples already, we'll look at those in detail in the following section, along with the principles that help us achieve those benefits.

Introducing the principles of a contract-driven data architecture

Building a contract-driven data architecture provides many benefits to both the data generators and consumers, and the wider organization. These benefits are achieved through these three principles:

- Automation
- Guidelines and guardrails
- Consistency

Let's look at each of these in turn.

Automation

There are several common tasks that need to be carried out on the data and the resources we use to manage it, no matter what that data is and who owns it. These tasks are great candidates to automate, reducing the effort the data generators need to spend managing the data.

The resources required for our data will almost always include the tables in the data warehouse. We can use the data contract to automate the creation and management of that table, for example, by creating the table when the contract is created and keeping the schema of the table in sync with the schema in the contract.

Other resources might include a topic in a streaming service such as Apache Kafka or Google Cloud Pub/Sub, the collection of metrics for SLOs, and the assignment of access controls. All of these can be automated too, using the data contract and the schema and metadata contained within it as the source of truth.

There are also regular actions we need to take *on* the data, which might include taking backups of the data, moving data to different storage engines based on its age, and anonymizing or deleting personally identifiable data as it exceeds its retention period.

Using the metadata defined in the data contract, we can easily build small services that automate these tasks. These services can be deployed alongside each contract and have sensible defaults, so most data generators never need to configure them.

We'll be looking at examples of implementing this automation in *Chapter 8, A Sample Implementation*.

Guidelines and guardrails

We want to enable data generators across the organization, but we can't expect everyone generating data to be experts in data contracts and other best practices. Instead, we can provide them with the tooling that guides them and take care of as many of these concerns for them as we can.

These act as our *guidelines and guardrails*. They help the users align with our contract-driven architecture by leading them in the right direction. They allow the data generators to focus on their data products and meeting the requirements of their consumers, knowing that if they use the supported tools and categorize the data accurately, they are complying with the organization's data management standards.

The guidelines and guardrails also allow the data generators to move *fast*. They don't need constant engagement and review from central data or privacy engineering teams, which become a bottleneck and slow down development speed across the organization.

These guidelines and guardrails are best implemented as part of the data generators day-to-day workflows. For example, **Continuous Integration (CI)** checks could ensure the data is categorized, and any field categorized as personal data has an anonymization strategy defined. We'll discuss these checks in more detail and provide further examples in *Chapter 10, Data Contracts in Practice*, in the *Monitoring and enforcing data contracts* section.

You won't be able to create guidelines for every question, or perfect guardrails that prevent all issues, and you'll need to keep adding and refining them as those issues arise. But they do significantly reduce the risks, without compromising on the agility and autonomy of the data generators.

Consistency

By providing this standard tooling to all data generators through data contracts, we're promoting greater consistency in how our data is managed, accessed, and consumed. Every data consumer knows how to discover data that is managed through a data contract. They know how to look up the expectations around that data, and how to find its owner. They know how the access controls are set up, and how to ask for the permissions they need.

Similarly, every data generator knows how their data and resources are being managed. They can switch between working on different datasets without losing context or having to learn new tools or a slightly different implementation of the same tools. When there is an incident, they know exactly where to look for their service configuration, to view their observability metrics, and recover data from their backups. This contract-driven tooling becomes the *golden path*. It is the only supported tooling and the default choice for data generators across the organization.

Achieving that greatly increases the return on investment in the tooling and justifies the investment in the data infrastructure team. The greater the usage, the fewer point solutions need to be built in different parts of the organization, and the time saved can be invested in generating business value.

However, this is only going to be achieved if the tooling is of the right quality and meets most of the needs of most of the data generators. The tooling needs to support those needs without creating unnecessary friction or reducing their autonomy.

The key to achieving that is to build the tooling in a way that data generators can self-serve themselves. Let's discuss why that is so important and how to provide that next.

Providing self-served data infrastructure

Data generators must be able to create and manage their data products with agility and autonomy if we are going to improve the accessibility of quality data that leads to valuable business outcomes.

To enable that, the tooling implemented as part of our contract-driven architecture needs to be self-servable by those data generators. There should be no waiting on a central data or operations teams for review, slowing the data generators down and becoming a bottleneck.

We can be confident in allowing this because we have implemented the guidelines and guardrails that manage the risks, as we discussed in the previous section. That allows us to *trust* our data generators, and by showing we trust them we are promoting a sense of *ownership* of the data. That sense of ownership automatically translates into a feeling of *responsibility and accountability* for the data, and the data products they are providing.

As we've discussed throughout this chapter, data contracts make it easy to build this tooling and have it driven by the schema and the metadata within the contract.

We can see how this works by looking at how data contracts have been implemented at GoCardless. The following code block shows an example data contract defined in Jsonnet, which is how we define the contracts at GoCardless:

```
{
  contract: new() {
    metadata+: {
      name: 'bank_account_information',
      description: 'Information on bank accounts used for ...',
    },
    schema+: {
      versions: [
        new_version('1', anonymisation_strategy.overwrite,
          [
            field(
              'bank_account_id',
              'Unique identifier for a specific bank account,
 following the standard GC ID format.',
              data_types.string,
              field_category.gocardless_internal,
```

```
                    is_personal_data.yes,
                    personal_data_identifier.indirect,
                    field_anonymisation_strategy.none,
                    required=true,
                    primary_key=true,
                ),
                field(
                    'account_balance',
                    'Payer\'s account balance. May be positive or
negative.',
                    data_types.double,
                    field_category.payer_confidential,
                    is_personal_data.yes,
                    personal_data_identifier.direct,
                    field_anonymisation_strategy.nilable
                ),
                field(
                    'account_holder_name',
                    'Payer\'s account holder name, as entered by the
payer.',
                    data_types.string,
                    field_category.payer_confidential,
                    is_personal_data.yes,
                    personal_data_identifier.direct,
                    field_anonymisation_strategy.hex
                ),
            ],
            [ ddrSubject('bank_accounts', 'bank_account_id') ],
        ) + withPubSub() + withBigQuery(),
        ],
    },
  },
}
```

That's all a data generator needs to do to create a data contract. The key part for this discussion is the following line:

```
+ withPubSub() + withBigQuery()
```

This is how the data generator can provision the resources and services they need, completely self-served. In this example, they are requesting a Google Cloud Pub/Sub topic and a Google BigQuery table. The data contract will be used to configure those with the correct schemas and keep those schemas in sync as the contract evolves.

Other services and resources are provisioned automatically and come with sensible defaults, including a data handling service to manage the life cycle of the data and a service that takes regular backups of the data. If they did want to configure these services, they could do so in the contract. For example, the following code changes the backups to weekly:

```
withBigQuery(backup_schedule="@weekly")
```

The data contract also integrates with several central services, including the data catalog and our observability platform.

Once they are happy with their data contract, they merge it to a Git repository – without central review – and those services and resources are created.

The following diagram shows how the different services and resources work together to give the data generator everything they need to create and manage their data:

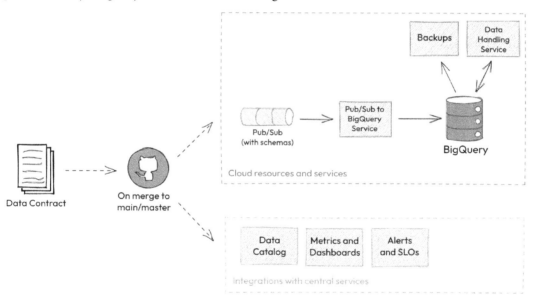

Figure 7.3 – The services and resources created and managed by the data contract

Looking forward, we expect to create all the tooling and services we will ever need in the same way, driven by the data contract and the metadata within it.

By having the ability to create and manage all these services and resources, and to do so through a self-serve interface, we allow our data generators to move fast and with autonomy as they focus on generating the quality data products our data consumers need.

Summary

In this chapter, we introduced the concept of a *contract-driven data architecture*. This is an architecture driven by data contracts and the metadata we define within them. We showed how powerful this idea is, and why we believe it's a step-change in how we build data platforms.

We use this pattern to build more generic data tooling, where instead of building similar pipelines as point solutions we can build tooling that doesn't mandate anything about the data and how it is structured if we have enough context about the data, defined as metadata in the data contract. When adopting this pattern, it's recommended to build a data infrastructure team, whose remit is to build this tooling for the adoption of all data generators, wherever they are in the organization.

To illustrate how this pattern is different from how we built platforms before, we walked through a case study of a previous service we implemented at GoCardless, the Data Platform Gateway, and how that wasn't as successful as we'd hoped. We showed how we learned about the importance of *autonomy*, and how that led to us adopting this architecture pattern.

We then looked in detail at the benefits of this architecture pattern, and how they are achieved by three principles: autonomy, guardrails, and consistency. Finally, we discussed how important it is that the tooling is self-servable, and how that is the key to promoting autonomy.

In the next chapter, we're going to see this concept in action as we look at a sample implementation of this architecture pattern, driven by data contracts.

Further reading

For more information on the topics covered in this chapter, please see the following resources:

- *Implementing Data Contracts at GoCardless*: `https://medium.com/gocardless-tech/implementing-data-contracts-at-gocardless-3b5c49074d13`

- *3 Things Our Software Engineers Love About Data Contracts*: `https://medium.com/gocardless-tech/3-things-our-software-engineers-love-about-data-contracts-3106e1f1602d`

- *The Data Engineer is dead, long live the (Data) Platform Engineer* by Robert Sahlin: `https://robertsahlin.substack.com/p/the-data-engineer-is-dead-long-live`

- *Data-First Stack as an Enabler for Data Products* by Animesh Kumar: `https://moderndata101.substack.com/p/data-first-stack-as-an-enabler-for`

- *Building Great Cloud Security Guardrails* by Rich Mogull: `https://devops.com/building-great-cloud-security-guardrails/`

- *How We Use Golden Paths to Solve Fragmentation in Our Software Ecosystem* by Gary Niemen `https://engineering.atspotify.com/2020/08/how-we-use-golden-paths-to-solve-fragmentation-in-our-software-ecosystem/`

- *Self Service Pattern*: `https://www.cnpatterns.org/infrastructure-cloud/self-service`

- *What is a Self-Service Infrastructure Platform?* by Romaric Philogène: `https://medium.com/@rphilogene/what-is-a-self-service-infrastructure-platform-726a8d0dc2e1`

A Sample Implementation

In this chapter, we'll walk through a sample implementation of data contracts. We'll use it to illustrate the concepts we have been learning about throughout the book and put what we have learned into practice.

We'll start by creating a YAML-based interface for the data generator to use to create a data contract. Then, using that data contract as the foundation, we'll provide a few examples of how we can use it to drive our contract-driven architecture.

Firstly, we'll create a table in our BigQuery data warehouse from the data contract, with a matching schema that will stay in sync with the contract as it evolves. We'll also introduce an **Infrastructure as Code (IaC)** tool to help us build this. Then we'll look at how we can create libraries for the data generators to aid the generation of data that matches the contract and conforms to the data quality checks we have defined in the contract.

Next, we'll explore how to populate a schema registry from the contract, and how that helps make our schemas accessible to any code that needs it. The schema registry also allows us to store multiple versions of a contract, and we'll use that functionality to help us manage the evolution of our data contracts. Finally, we'll show how we can implement contract-driven tooling, using an anonymization service as an example.

By the end of this chapter, you'll have seen how easy and powerful it is to implement a data-contract-driven architecture.

In this chapter, we're going to cover the following main topics:

- Creating a data contract
- Providing the interfaces to the data
- Creating libraries for data generators
- Populating a central schema registry
- Implementing contract-driven tooling

Technical requirements

You can find all the code for this chapter in the `Chapter08` directory in the GitHub repository at `https://github.com/PacktPublishing/Driving-Data-Quality-with-Data-Contracts`.

To follow along with the code samples in this chapter, download the code from GitHub. Ensure you have Python version 3.9.12 or above installed on your local machine, and then run the following commands from the `Chapter08` directory to install the dependencies in a virtual environment:

```
$ python3 -m venv venv
$ source venv/bin/activate
$ pip install -r requirements.txt
```

You'll also need a Google Cloud account. If you don't have one already, you can sign up at `https://cloud.google.com`. Once created, you will need to ensure you have permission to create BigQuery datasets and tables in your project by following the instructions at `https://cloud.google.com/bigquery/docs/access-control`.

Next, install the `gcloud` CLI by following the instructions at `https://cloud.google.com/sdk/docs/install`, and initialize and authenticate the CLI as documented at `https://cloud.google.com/sdk/docs/initializing`.

The actions we will take in this chapter will not incur any charges.

We'll also be using Pulumi (`https://www.pulumi.com`) in this chapter. Install the `pulumi` CLI by following the instructions at `https://www.pulumi.com/docs/get-started/install/`.

Finally, we'll use Docker to run services locally. Install Docker Desktop from `https://docs.docker.com/desktop/`.

Creating a data contract

We'll start by defining a specification for data generators to create a data contract. We'll discuss why we have chosen to define it in this way, and how it acts as the foundation of our sample implementation.

We'll be using this data contract to drive the contract-driven architecture we'll be building out in this chapter. It will be the foundation that drives the following resources and services:

- A BigQuery table, acting as the interface to the data.
- Code libraries for the data generators to use, by converting our data contract to JSON Schema and using existing open source libraries.
- A schema registry, so the schemas are available to others. Again, we used our JSON Schema representation of the data contract to interact with that.

- An anonymization service, which uses the data contract directly to anonymize some data.

The following diagram shows how each of these resources is driven by the data contract, which is highlighted:

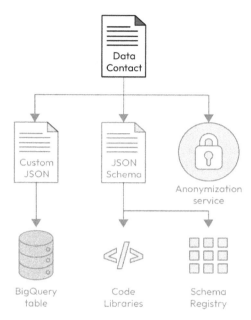

Figure 8.1 – Using the data contract to drive our contract-driven architecture

As we discussed in *Chapter 6, What Makes Up a Data Contract*, there are many ways we can implement this interface. From using an existing schema definition language such as Apache Avro and Protocol Buffers, to higher-level definition languages such as YAML and Jsonnet, to writing in code such as Python and TypeScript.

For this example, we'll be using a custom interface captured in YAML. YAML is a popular and well-known definition language that is easy for humans to read and write while still being machine-readable. Its flexibility also allows us to capture as much metadata as we need to implement the features we will be building throughout this chapter. This includes the following:

- A schema holding the fields, their data types, and whether they are required or optional
- Optional validation rules for the fields
- An anonymization strategy for the data

The following code block from `contracts/Customer.yaml` shows a data contract for our Customer record:

```yaml
name: Customer
description: A customer of our e-commerce website.
owner: product-team@data-contracts.com
version: 1
fields:
  id:
    type: string
    description: The unique identifier for the customer.
    required: true
  name:
    type: string
    description: The name of the customer.
    required: true
    anonymization_strategy: hex
  email:
    type: string
    description: The email address of the customer.
    pattern: "^[a-zA-Z0-9._%+-]+@[a-zA-Z0-9.-]+\\.[a-zA-Z]{2,}$"
    required: true
    anonymization_strategy: email
  language:
    type: string
    description: The language preference of the customer.
    enum: [en, fr, es]
```

This will be all our data generators need to do to create the data contract. From this, we will be able to provision the resources and services using the patterns described in *Chapter 7, A Contract-Driven Data Architecture.*

It's important the data contract is machine-readable, and there are libraries that make it easy to read YAML in all the major programming languages. The following code from `parse_contract.py` shows us parsing the data contract in Python and extracting some of the metadata from it:

```python
import yaml

with open("contracts/Customer.yaml", "r") as stream:
    contract = yaml.safe_load(stream)

print(
    f'Successfully parsed the `{contract["name"]}` contract, which is
owned by `{contract["owner"]}`.')
```

You can run this and view the output as follows:

```
$ ./parse-contract.py
Successfully parsed the `Customer` contract, which is owned by
`product-team@data-contracts.com`.
```

We can take this a little further by implementing checks to validate the data contract. To take a simple example, we can mandate every data contract has an owner by adding the following lines to our code, which are implemented in validate_contract.py:

```
if 'owner' not in contract:
    raise ValueError(f'`{contract["name"]}` contract does not have an
owner')
```

Running that code against the contracts/Customer-invalid.yaml data contract, where we've removed the owner field, will throw an error, as follows:

```
$ ./validate_contract.py
Traceback (most recent call last):
  File "Driving-Data-Quality-with-Data-Contracts/Chapter08/validate_
contract.py", line 7, in <module>
    raise ValueError(f'`{contract["name"]}` contract does not have an
owner')
ValueError: `Customer` contract does not have an owner
```

We can obviously take this further and add as many validations as we need. A script such as this can then be used to fail builds or continuous integration checks, ensuring the correctness and consistency of our data contracts.

We now have a way to define a data contract, but we're not doing much with it yet. Next, let's look at how we can use the data contract to supply an interface to the data through the provision of a table in a data warehouse.

Providing the interfaces to the data

In this section, we'll use the data contract to provision a Google BigQuery table. This will act as the **interface** to the data, through which the data generators will make their data available to the data consumers. We'll learn how to use the contract and its schema to dynamically provision and manage those resources, keeping them in sync with the data contract.

This BigQuery table is the first of our contract-driven resources. To create it, we'll need to convert our data contract to a custom JSON format that defines a BigQuery table and its schema (https://cloud.google.com/bigquery/docs/reference/rest/v2/tables#TableSchema), as highlighted in the following diagram:

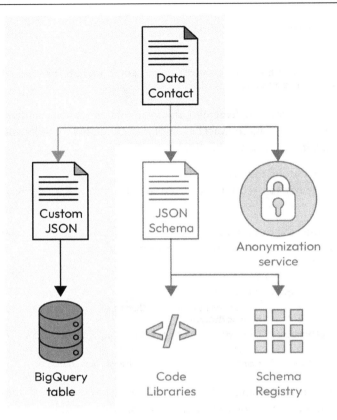

Figure 8.2 – Using the data contract to define and create a BigQuery table

We'll also need a way to send that JSON to the Google Cloud APIs, which will then create the table. To do that, we are going to make use of an IaC tool, so we'll introduce that first before showing how we can use it to provision these resources.

In the following subsections, we're going to cover the following topics:

- Introducing IaC
- Creating the interfaces from the data contract

Introducing IaC

IaC tools enable us to provision and manage resources through code. The result of running that code defines the desired state, and these tools provision and configure the infrastructure accordingly.

There are several benefits to IaC, including the flexibility to describe complex infrastructure in a consistent and well-documented format. It promotes reusability and testability, and the code is typically stored using a version control system such as Git. Popular IaC tools include Terraform (`https://www.terraform.io`) and Ansible (`https://www.ansible.com`).

Much like a data contract, there are many languages you can use to define your infrastructure as code, including definition languages such as JSON and YAML and programming languages such as TypeScript and Python.

For this example, we'll be using Pulumi (`https://www.pulumi.com`) as our IaC tool. Pulumi allows us to define our infrastructure using programming languages such as Python, which makes it flexible and enables the integration of IaC into other workflows:

1. To illustrate this, the following Python code snippet from `pulumi_introduction/__main__.py` shows how to create a BigQuery dataset and table using Pulumi:

```python
import pulumi
from pulumi_gcp import bigquery

default_dataset = bigquery.Dataset(
    "defaultDataset",
    dataset_id="pulumi_introduction",
    friendly_name="Pulumi Introduction",
    description="This is an example description",
)
default_table = bigquery.Table(
    "defaultTable",
    dataset_id=default_dataset.dataset_id,
    table_id="my_table",
    deletion_protection=False,
    schema="""[
{
    "name": "id",
    "type": "STRING",
    "mode": "REQUIRED",
    "description": "The ID"
},
{
    "name": "state",
    "type": "STRING",
    "description": "State where the head office is located"
}
]
""")
```

2. To run this, you first need to edit `Pulumi.introduction.yaml` and set the Google Cloud project you are using by changing the following highlighted configuration parameter:

```
config:
  gcp:project: my-google-project-2468
```

3. Next, we need to tell Pulumi where to store state. It compares this state against the infrastructure, so it knows what changes to make. Pulumi supports a few different backends in which it will store the state, including cloud storage services such as AWS S3 and Google Cloud Storage, as well as the Pulumi cloud. See `https://www.pulumi.com/docs/intro/concepts/state/` for more details.

4. To keep things simple, we'll store state on our local filesystem. Run the following command to log in to Pulumi with local state:

```
$ pulumi login --local
Logged in to AC1234 as andrewjones (file://~)
```

5. Now let's ask Pulumi to create the BigQuery dataset and table by running the following from the `pulumi_introduction` directory:

```
$ pulumi up
```

You'll be prompted to enter a new stack name. A *stack* is an isolated instance of a Pulumi program. More details on stacks can be found at `https://www.pulumi.com/docs/intro/concepts/stack/`.

6. Enter `introduction` at the prompt and hit *Enter*. You will be asked for a passphrase and after entering one, you'll see the following output:

```
Previewing update (introduction):
    Type                    Name                         Plan
      Info
+   pulumi:pulumi:Stack     data-contracts-introduction  create
+   ├─ gcp:bigquery:Dataset defaultDataset               create
+   └─ gcp:bigquery:Table   defaultTable                 create

Do you want to perform this update?  [Use arrows to move, type
to filter]
  yes
> no
  details
```

Pulumi has now run our Python code and found the BigQuery dataset and table resources we defined. It has queried the Google Cloud APIs and found they do not already exist, and so is telling us that it intends to create them, along with the stack as it's our first time running against it. You can see more details on the resources we're provisioning by selecting `details`, which will show the properties we have defined.

7. Let's go ahead and create these resources by choosing `yes` from the prompt. You'll see the following output:

```
Do you want to perform this update? yes
Updating (introduction):
     Type                    Name
Status
     pulumi:pulumi:Stack      data-contracts-introduction
+    ├─
gcp:bigquery:Dataset   defaultDataset              created
(0.98s)
+    └─
gcp:bigquery:Table     defaultTable                created
(0.83s)

Resources:
  + 3 created
```

Well done, you've provisioned some resources using Pulumi!

8. Let's confirm by looking at the Google Cloud console. Open your web browser and go to `https://console.cloud.google.com/bigquery`. Log in and, if needed, select the correct project from the dropdown. You'll then see the following screen, showing the dataset on the left (`pulumi_introduction`) and the table (`my_table`), with the correct schema applied to the table:

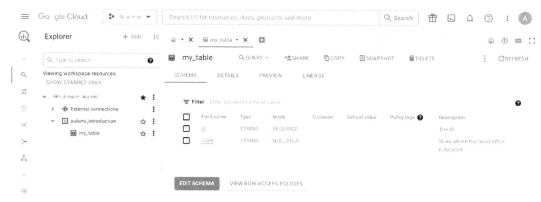

Figure 8.3 – The Google Cloud console showing the BigQuery resources we provisioned with Pulumi

That concludes our introduction to Pulumi. We have successfully defined our infrastructure as code. We ran that code with Pulumi, which provisioned the resources as we defined them.

9. We no longer need these resources, so let's remove them by running `pulumi destroy`, choosing `yes` when asked whether we want to destroy these resources:

```
$ pulumi destroy
Previewing destroy (introduction):
        Type                        Name                          Plan
-       pulumi:pulumi:Stack         data-contracts-introduction   delete
-       ├─ gcp:bigquery:Table     defaultTable                  delete
-       └─ gcp:bigquery:Dataset   defaultDataset                delete


Resources:
    - 3 to delete

Do you want to perform this destroy? yes
Destroying (introduction):
        Type                    Name
Status
-       pulumi:pulumi:Stack        data-contracts-
introduction   deleted
-       ├─
gcp:bigquery:Table      defaultTable                    deleted
(0.77s)
-       └─
gcp:bigquery:Dataset    defaultDataset                  deleted
(0.42s)


Resources:
    - 3 deleted
```

Let's look now at how we can use Pulumi to create the interfaces to our data from the data contract.

Creating the interfaces from the data contract

We now have a way to define a data contract, through our custom YAML definition, and an infrastructure as code tool to programmatically define and manage infrastructure via Pulumi. Let's combine them to create an interface for our data.

In this example, we'll be creating a Google BigQuery table to act as the interface. BigQuery is a popular data warehouse, and data contracts are often used to populate and manage data in a data warehouse to make it available to data consumers, including BI analysts and data scientists.

For this section, we'll be using the Pulumi application defined in the `pulumi` directory. As before, we need to set the Google Cloud project to the one we'll using by changing the following highlighted configuration parameter in `Pulumi.contracts.yaml`:

```
config:
  gcp:project: my-google-project-2468
```

As we discussed in *Chapter 6, What Makes Up a Data Contract*, one of the benefits of data contracts is the ability to convert the contract into different formats, depending on what we want to integrate with. If we capture the right metadata in the contract, we can integrate with any system we like.

To illustrate that point, we'll be doing the following:

- Creating a BigQuery schema from our data contract

- Using Pulumi to create and manage our BigQuery table

Creating a BigQuery schema from our data contract

As we saw in our Pulumi introduction earlier, BigQuery schemas are defined through a custom JSON document. All we need to do is generate that JSON from the data contract.

We've created a `DataContract` class to hold our data-contract-related code, which you can find in `lib/data_contracts.py`. The relevant code for this example is shown in the following code snippet, and simply converts our YAML-based data contract into the custom JSON used to define a BigQuery schema by iterating over the `fields` items in our contract and extracting the required metadata:

```
bq_schema = []
for name, metadata in self.fields().items():
    schema = {
        'name': name,
        'type': metadata['type'].upper(),
        'description': metadata['description']
    }
    if 'required' in metadata and metadata['required'] is True:
        schema['mode'] = 'REQUIRED'
    bq_schema.append(schema)

return json.dumps(bq_schema, indent=2)
```

We'll use the output of this code in the next step, where we'll create our data contracts-backed BigQuery table.

Using Pulumi to create and manage our BigQuery table

Now we have the schema represented in the BigQuery JSON specification, we can call this from Pulumi to define the BigQuery table resources, as shown in the following code snippet from `Pulumi/__main__.py`:

```
data_contract = DataContract("../contracts/Customer.yaml")
customer_table = bigquery.Table("customerTable",
    dataset_id=dataset.dataset_id,
```

```
table_id=data_contract.name(),
deletion_protection=False,
schema=data_contract.bigquery_schema())
```

Let's run this through Pulumi by running `pulumi up` in the `pulumi` directory. You'll be asked whether you want to use our existing `introduction` stack or create a new one. Since this is a new Pulumi application, create a new stack called `contracts` and enter a new passphrase for it. Pulumi will then show you the resources it plans to provision:

```
$ pulumi up
Previewing update (contracts):
    Type                       Name                     Plan
+   pulumi:pulumi:Stack        data-contracts-contracts create
+   ├─ gcp:bigquery:Dataset    dataProductsDataset      create
+   └─ gcp:bigquery:Table      customerTable            create


Resources:
    + 3 to create
```

You can choose `details` from the prompt to see the schema definition Pulumi will use for the table, represented in BigQuery's JSON format, as follows:

```
schema            : (json) [
    [0]: {
        description: "The unique identifier for the customer."
        mode       : "REQUIRED"
        name       : "id"
        type       : "STRING"
    }
    [1]: {
        description: "The name of the customer."
        mode       : "REQUIRED"
        name       : "name"
        type       : "STRING"
    }
    [2]: {
        description: "The email address of the customer."
        mode       : "REQUIRED"
        name       : "email"
        type       : "STRING"
    }
    [3]: {
        description: "The language preference of the customer."
        name       : "language"
```

```
        type      :  "STRING"
    }
]
```

That looks as expected! So, choose `yes` from the prompt to provision the resources. When Pulumi has finished, open your web browser and go to `https://console.cloud.google.com/bigquery`. You'll then see the following screen, showing the dataset on the left (`data_products`) and the table (`Customers`), with the contract-driven schema applied to the table:

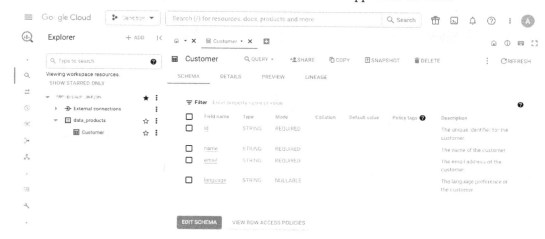

Figure 8.4 – The Google Cloud console showing the BigQuery resources we provisioned from the data contract definition, through Pulumi

That was easy! With just a few lines of code, we're able to create a BigQuery table from our data contract. Feel free to play around and see what happens as you make changes to the data contract, maybe by adding a new field. Run `pulumi up` again and see how it keeps the table's schema in sync with the data contract. When you are finished with this example, you can remove the resources with `pulumi destroy`.

This example illustrates how powerful it is to create and manage resources driven by the data contract, and how easy it is to do so. We can apply this pattern to any kind of resource, including alternative data warehouses such as Snowflake and Amazon Redshift.

We can also supply different interfaces to the data, including for streaming use cases. For example, we could use Pulumi to create a Google Cloud Pub/Sub topic to act as a contract-driven interface for streaming data and apply a schema to that topic by converting our data contract to Avro or Protocol Buffers (`https://cloud.google.com/pubsub/docs/schemas`).

Refer to *Chapter 7, A Contract-Driven Data Architecture*, for more examples based on this architecture pattern.

Now we've created a BigQuery table to act as an interface for the data, we want to make it easy for the data generators to write the data to that table. Let's see how we can generate libraries for them, using the data contract.

Creating libraries for data generators

As well as making it easy for data generators to provision and manage resources, we can also make it easy for them to generate and publish their data to those resources. One way to do that is to supply some client libraries. These can help with data conversion, perform validation checks, or perform custom logic that helps ensure data generated by different services is consistent.

These client libraries are also useful to the consumers of the data, helping with the deserialization of data or the deduction of any custom logic.

You could decide to implement these libraries yourself, using the raw data contract as the input. Alternatively, you can convert the data contract into an open source format and use the existing ecosystem.

That's what we'll be doing. In this section, we'll convert our data contract to JSON Schema (`https://json-schema.org`) and learn how to use existing libraries to validate our data, as highlighted in the following diagram:

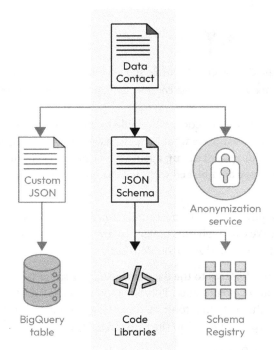

Figure 8.5 – Converting the data contract to JSON Schema to create libraries for data generators

We'll start by writing the code to generate a JSON Schema from our data contract. This is easy to do, with some code that iterates over the `fields` items from our contract and extracts the required metadata. The relevant code from `lib/data_contracts.py` is shown in the following snippet:

```
properties = {}
required = []
for name, metadata in self.fields().items():
    properties[name] = {
        'description': metadata['description'],
        'type': metadata['type']
    }
    if 'enum' in metadata:
        properties[name]['enum'] = metadata['enum']
    if 'pattern' in metadata:
        properties[name]['pattern'] = metadata['pattern']

    if 'required' in metadata and metadata['required'] is True:
        required.append(name)

schema = {
    "$schema": "https://json-schema.org/draft/2020-12/schema",
    "title": self.name(),
    "description": self.contract['description'],
    "type": "object",
    "properties": properties,
    "required": required
}
return schema
```

You can use this code to generate a full JSON Schema representation of our data contract by running the following script from the `Chapter08` directory:

```
$ ./generate-json-schema.py
Written JSON Schema of `Customer` data contract to `customer.schema.
json`
```

The full JSON Schema is written to `customer.schema.json`, and a snippet of that schema follows:

```
{
  "title": "Customer",
  "description": "A customer of our e-commerce
website.",  "properties": {
    "id": {
      "description": "The unique identifier for the customer.",
      "type": "string"
```

```
    },
    "email": {
      "description": "The email address of the customer.",
      "type": "string",
      "pattern": "^[a-zA-Z0-9._%+-]+@[a-zA-Z0-9.-]+\\.[a-zA-Z]{2,}$"
    },
  },
  "required": ["id", "name", "email"]
}
```

As a popular open format, we can use this JSON Schema in a wide variety of applications and use various open source libraries, as listed at https://json-schema.org/implementations. One of those libraries is the Python jsonschema library (https://pypi.org/project/jsonschema/), which can be used to validate data against a JSON Schema in just one line of code, as shown in the following code snippet from validate-data.py:

```
validate(event, data_contract.json_schema())
```

In validate-data.py we have created several example events to show this validation in action and run them through the validate function from jsonschema. Run it as follows and see the output, a sample of which is shown in the following code block:

```
$ ./validate-data.py
Successfully validated event {'id': 'DC12', 'name': 'Andrew', 'email':
'andrew@data-contracts.com', 'language': 'en'}
Successfully validated event {'id': 'DC13', 'name': 'Deborah',
'email': 'deborah@data-contracts.com'}
Error validating event {'id': 'DC14', 'name': 'Bukayo', 'language':
'en'}
'email' is a required property
Error validating event {'id': 'DC15', 'name': 'Bukayo', 'email':
'bukayo', 'language': 'en'}
'bukayo' does not match '^[a-zA-Z0-9._%+-]+@[a-zA-Z0-9.-]+\\.[a-zA-Z]
{2,}$'
Error validating event {'id': 'DC16', 'name': 'Vivianne', 'email':
'vivianne@data-contracts.com', 'language': 'nl'}
'nl' is not one of ['en', 'fr', 'es']
```

By converting our data contract to an existing open format, we have quickly been able to produce a client library that data generators can use to perform validation on their data, both when developing their applications and in production. They can then act on this result, for example, by raising an alert for them to investigate, preventing this data from affecting downstream users.

To do this, we need to make the data contracts, or a representation of the contracts, available to code in various places. Let's look next at how a schema registry can help with that.

Populating a central schema registry

We've just seen how, by having our schemas accessible to our code, we can make use of a variety of libraries to ease the generation and consumption of data. That relies on having easy access to those schemas, wherever you need them. In this section, we'll learn how to populate a schema registry from our data contract, making our schemas available to any service or code, at any time.

Again, we'll be converting our data contract to JSON Schema, then using that to populate the schema registry, as highlighted in the following diagram:

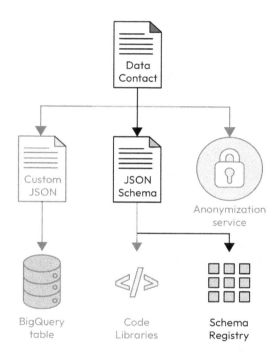

Figure 8.6 – Converting the data contract to JSON Schema to populate a schema registry

We discussed schema registries and their benefits in *Chapter 6, What Makes Up a Data Contract*, under the *Using a schema registry as the source of truth* section. One of the benefits we mentioned is that they act as a central store for the schemas, so any application can access them. They also act as a source of truth, so when one application refers to *version 1* of our `Customer` schema, that needs to be the same schema as the next application that refers to it.

Many schema registries also support schema evolution. They allow the storing of many versions of a particular schema and perform compatibility checks when we try to register a new version of that schema. We'll also look at how those checks work in practice.

In this section, we're going to cover the following topics:

- Registering a schema with the Confluent schema registry
- Managing schema evolution

While in this section we are focusing on the capabilities a schema registry provides, this is also a good example of integrating data contracts with central services. Other central services such as data catalogs, privacy systems, and BI tools can be populated from a data contract in much the same way, particularly if they support open standards such as JSON Schema.

Registering a schema with the Confluent schema registry

Let's start by looking at how to register a schema with a schema registry, using the data contract as the source of that schema. There are many implementations of a schema registry. For this example, we'll be using the Confluent schema registry (`https://docs.confluent.io/platform/current/schema-registry/`), as it is one of the few that has native support for JSON Schema, including schema evolution:

1. We'll be using Docker to run the schema registry on our local machines, along with its dependencies (Apache Kafka and Apache ZooKeeper). To start the schema registry, run the following from the `Chapter08/schema_registry/` directory:

   ```
   $ docker-compose up
   ```

2. It may take a few minutes to start up. We can confirm the registry is available by running the following in a different terminal window, which lists the schema types supported by the schema registry, and should include JSON, confirming JSON Schema support:

   ```
   $ curl http://localhost:8081/schemas/types
   ["JSON","PROTOBUF","AVRO"]
   ```

3. Let's upload our JSON Schema representation of the data contract to the schema registry. We're using the Confluent Python libraries to do this in just a few lines of code. Run the script with the following command:

   ```
   $ ./create-schema.py
   Registered schema `Customer` with ID of 1
   ```

   Our schema is now registered in the schema registry!

4. Every schema has a unique ID, which we can use to fetch the schema by calling the following API:

   ```
   $ curl http://localhost:8081/schemas/ids/1/schema
   {"$schema":"https://json-schema.org/draft/2020-12/
   schema","title":"Customer","description":"A customer of ...
   ```

5. We may not always know the ID of the schema we want. Most often, we will want to retrieve a schema based on the name of it (or *subject*, as the Confluent schema registry calls them). We can find the subjects known to the schema registry by calling the following API:

```
$ curl http://localhost:8081/subjects
["Customer"]
```

6. The schema registry has support for storing many versions of a schema. We can see how many versions are registered for a subject as follows:

```
$ curl http://localhost:8081/subjects/Customer/versions
[1]
```

7. For now, we only have one version of our Customer schema. Given the name of the subject and the version number, we can now get the schema we want without using the ID by calling the following API:

```
$ curl http://localhost:8081/subjects/Customer/versions/1/schema
{"$schema":"https://json-schema.org/draft/2020-12/
schema","title":"Customer","description":"A customer of ...
```

8. Or, if we only care about fetching the latest schema, we can use the latest instead of the version number, as follows:

```
$ curl http://localhost:8081/subjects/Customer/versions/latest/
schema
{"$schema":"https://json-schema.org/draft/2020-12/
schema","title":"Customer","description":"A customer of ...
```

The support for multiple versions of a schema allows us to manage the evolution of those schemas. Let's see why that is important and how to make use of these features next.

Managing schema evolution

As we discussed in *Chapter 6*, *What Makes Up a Data Contract*, under the *Evolving your data over time* section, our data contracts need to evolve over time to support the evolution of our organization's data.

The Confluent schema registry helps us manage this evolution by storing the history of all the versions we've had for a schema and by providing APIs that let us test the compatibility of a schema against those earlier versions:

1. Let's start by adding a new optional field to our Customer schema. This is a *non-breaking* change. By this, we mean the change can be implemented by the generators without affecting any existing consumers. The generators can start populating the field, and existing consumers who are using the earlier version simply ignore that field.

2. In `contracts/Customer-v2.yaml`, we've added a new optional `country` field to the schema. No other changes to the contract have been made. We can see the difference by running the following command:

```
$ diff -u contracts/Customer.yaml contracts/Customer-v2.yaml
--- ../contracts/Customer.yaml      2023-04-25 17:40:18
+++ ../contracts/Customer-v2.yaml      2023-05-02 17:26:51
@@ -24,3 +24,6 @@
    type: string
    description: The language preference of the customer.
    enum: [en, fr, es]
+  country:
+    type: string
+    description: The country the customer resides in.
```

3. Let's register this schema as an updated version in our schema registry. From the `schema_registry` directory, run the following script, which is identical to the one we used to create the schema, except using `Customer-v2.yaml` as the source:

```
$ ./update-schema-v2.py
Updated schema `Customer` with ID of 2
```

4. Once again, we have a unique ID for this schema, which can be used to retrieve it. We can also run the following command to see that the schema registry has saved this as an updated version:

```
$ curl http://localhost:8081/subjects/Customer/versions
[1,2]
```

5. The schema registry also stores this as the latest version of the schema, so it can be retrieved as follows:

```
$ curl http://localhost:8081/subjects/Customer/versions/latest/
schema
{"$schema":"https://json-schema.org/draft/2020-12/
schema","title":"Customer","description":"A customer of ...
```

So, we now have an updated version of the schema. As a non-breaking change that doesn't affect existing consumers, we were able to introduce this change with *low friction*. We may not even need to notify our consumers, and they can continue using the earlier version until they need access to that new field.

6. Now let's look at how the schema registry can help us manage *breaking changes*. In `contracts/Customer-v3-incompatible.yaml`, we have removed the `email` field, as shown by running the following command:

```
$ diff -u contracts/Customer-v2.yaml contracts/Customer-v3-
incompatible.yaml
```

```
--- contracts/Customer-v2.yaml     2023-05-08 15:22:45
+++ contracts/Customer-v3-incompatible.yaml     2023-05-08
15:22:51
@@ -12,12 +12,6 @@
    description: The name of the customer.
    required: true
    anonymization_strategy: hex
-  email:
-    type: string
-    description: The email address of the customer.
-    pattern: "^[a-zA-Z0-9._%+-]+@[a-zA-Z0-9.-]+\\.[a-zA-Z]
{2,}$"
-    required: true
-    anonymization_strategy: email
  language:
    type: string
    description: The language preference of the customer.
```

Any consumer using this field would be affected instantly by this change if it were to be made without them first updating their code or reports. Depending on the data and its importance to the organization, that impact could be wide-ranging and affect many consumers. It could potentially affect business-critical applications that serve our customers and perhaps directly affect our revenue.

When we register this schema as an updated version of our Customer subject, the schema registry will first run some checks to ensure the schema is compatible with the earlier versions. If it fails these checks, the schema will not be registered, and an error will be returned.

7. Let's see this in action by running the update-schema-v3-incompatible.py script. This script is the same as the others except using the Customer-v3-incompatible.yaml contract as the source. The output of that script follows:

```
$ ./update-schema-v3-incompatible.py
confluent_kafka.schema_registry.error.SchemaRegistryError:
Schema being registered is incompatible with an earlier schema
for subject "Customer", details: [Found incompatible change:
Difference{jsonPath='#/properties/email', type=PROPERTY_ADDED_
TO_OPEN_CONTENT_MODEL}] (HTTP status code 409, SR code 409)
```

These compatibility checking features provided by the schema registry can be used to prevent these changes from being deployed to production and affecting consumers of our data contract, for example, as a continuous integration check.

As we discussed in *Chapter 4, Bringing Data Consumers and Generators Closer Together*, under the *Managing the evolution of data* section, when making breaking changes like this, we need to first discuss a migration plan with our data consumers. Often, that will include publishing the data side by side for a period while the consumers update their code and reports, so we will want both versions of the schema in the schema registry. While this does add friction, this is *intentional*. It's the trade-off we are choosing to make where we promote stability over ease of change.

The Confluent schema registry doesn't have support for publishing a new line of versions against an existing subject. So instead, we would need to register the schema as a new subject and use a naming convention, so we know it is an updated version of the same event.

For example, we could have registered our first `Customer` schema as `Customer.v1`, with the *major* version as part of the subject name. Each of our compatible versions could then be referenced as *minor* versions of that contract. In our case, we would have `v1.1` and `v1.2`. The version that introduced the breaking change would then be a new subject named `Customer.v2`, a version `v2.1` of that contract.

With this strategy, our data contracts follow **semantic versioning** (`https://semver.org`), a versioning scheme widely adopted in software development with clear rules around the meaning of a major and a minor change. (Although we aren't using patch numbers here, if we wanted to, we could use them to track changes such as documentation and other non-schema updates. Otherwise, we don't really need them.)

That completes our look at how to use a schema registry with data contracts, and how they make the schemas accessible through a rich API. We've also seen how we can use the schema registry to store many versions of a contract, and how we can use compatibility checks implemented in the schema registry to manage schema evolution.

8. We no longer need our schema registry, so we can remove the resources by running the following command:

```
$ docker-compose down
```

The schema registry helps our data generators and data consumers by managing our schemas and making them accessible. But from the contract itself, there's even more we can build. Next, we'll be looking at how we can implement this contract-driven tooling.

Implementing contract-driven tooling

The final part of our sample implementation looks at how we can easily implement tooling driven by the data contract, using the example of a data anonymization service.

As we discussed in *Chapter 7, A Contract-Driven Data Architecture*, one of the key benefits of data contracts is that we can use the metadata we capture to build generic data tooling. These tools don't know or care about the data itself or how it is structured. If it knows enough *about* the data, it can take the right action.

As the data contract itself is machine-readable, and we're writing custom code, we can use it directly from this service, as highlighted in the following diagram:

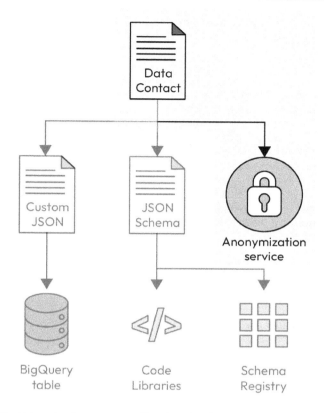

Figure 8.7 – Using the data contract directly to implement an anonymization service

As with all the examples shown in this chapter, the code is simple. The following code from anonymize.py shows a simple anonymization function driven by the contract:

```
def anonymize(event: dict, data_contract: DataContract):
    anonymized = event.copy()
    for name, metadata in data_contract.fields().items():
        if 'anonymization_strategy' in metadata:
            if metadata['anonymization_strategy'] == 'email':
                anonymized[name] = f"anonymized+{event['id']}@data-
contracts.com"
            if metadata['anonymization_strategy'] == 'hex':
                anonymized[name] = event[name].encode("utf-8").hex()

    return anonymized
```

This code will work on any data contract and anonymize the data according to the rules in that data contract. It can be executed as follows:

```
$ ./anonymize.py
Anonymizing:        {'id': 'DC12', 'name': 'Andrew', 'email': 'andrew@
data-contracts.com', 'language': 'en'}
{'id': 'DC12', 'name': '416e64726577', 'email': 'anonymized+DC12@data-
contracts.com', 'language': 'en'}
Anonymizing:        {'id': 'DC13', 'name': 'Deborah', 'email':
'deborah@data-contracts.com'}
{'id': 'DC13', 'name': '4465626f726168', 'email': 'anonymized+DC13@
data-contracts.com'}
Anonymizing:        {'id': 'DC14', 'name': 'Bukayo', 'email': 'bukayo@
data-contracts.com', 'language': 'en'}
{'id': 'DC14', 'name': '42756b61796f', 'email': 'anonymized+DC14@data-
contracts.com', 'language': 'en'}
```

While this is a simple example, it does illustrate the ease with which such tools can be built and applied to all data that is managed with a data contract. It really is possible to build any data tooling in the same way, including the following:

- Implementing data quality checks
- Automating data access controls
- Collecting and reporting on **service-level agreements** (SLAs)
- Sending the data on to other systems or third parties
- Taking regular backups of the data

And by providing this tooling for data generators, they can focus on generating quality data that meets the needs of their consumers and not spend time implementing their own similar tooling for common tasks.

With this, we've completed our sample implementation of a data-contract-backed architecture, by using our data contract as a foundation to drive the following resources and services:

- A BigQuery table, acting as the interface to the data.
- Code libraries for the data generators to use, by converting our data contract to JSON Schema and using existing open source libraries.
- A schema registry, so the schemas are available to others. Again, we used our JSON Schema representation of the data contract to interact with that.
- An anonymization service, which used the data contract directly to anonymize some data.

The following diagram shows how we built each of these just from the data contract:

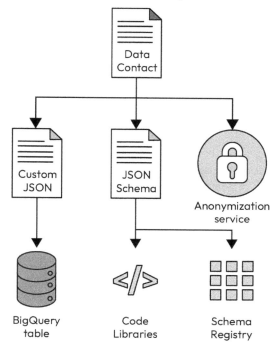

Figure 8.8 – Our sample implementation of a data contract-driven architecture

Each of these is just an example of what can be built with data-contracts, through a contract-driven architecture. Any data tooling or integration can be built in much the same way. Feel free to take this sample implementation and see what else you can build!

Summary

In this chapter, we walked through a sample implementation of a data-contract-driven architecture and used that to illustrate the concepts we have been learning throughout the book and show them in action. We started by defining a contract in a custom YAML-based interface, and used that to drive a few different applications and services.

The first of those was a BigQuery table, which acts as the interface between the data generators and the consumers. We introduced an IaC tool called Pulumi and showed how it can be used to create and manage resources driven by the data contract.

We then showed how, by converting our data contract to JSON Schema, an open standard, we can easily produce libraries to help the data generators publish data that matches the schema and passes the data quality checks we defined.

That same JSON Schema was then used to populate a schema registry. We showed how that allows the schemas to be easily accessible through its rich API and also looked at its versioning features to help us manage schema evolution.

Finally, we gave an example of an anonymization tool driven by the data contract to show how easy it is to build tools that, driven only by the data contract, can act on any data of any shape and size to perform its task, allowing the data generators to focus solely on generating quality data for their consumers.

Of course, this sample implementation can only illustrate the concepts and is unlikely to be something you can copy directly. So, in the next chapter, we'll discuss how to implement data contracts in *your* organization.

Further reading

For more information on the topics covered in this chapter, please see the following resources:

- *Implementing Data Contracts at GoCardless*: https://medium.com/gocardless-tech/implementing-data-contracts-at-gocardless-3b5c49074d13
- *What is a Self-Service Infrastructure Platform?* by Romaric Philogène: https://medium.com/@rphilogene/what-is-a-self-service-infrastructure-platform-726a8d0dc2e1
- *The Pulumi Book* by Christian Nunciato: https://leanpub.com/pulumi
- https://json-schema.org
- *Understanding JSON Schema Compatibility* by Robert Yokota: https://yokota.blog/2021/03/29/understanding-json-schema-compatibility/
- *The Many Amazing Uses of JSON Schema: Client-side Validation* by Phil Sturgeon: https://medium.com/apis-you-wont-hate/the-many-amazing-uses-of-json-schema-client-side-validation-c78a11fbde45
- *Data Contracts for Schema Registry*: https://docs.confluent.io/platform/current/schema-registry/fundamentals/data-contracts.html
- *Major.Minor.Patch. An illustrated guide to semantic versioning*: https://medium.com/fiverr-engineering/major-minor-patch-a5298e2e1798

9

Implementing Data Contracts in Your Organization

In this chapter, we'll look at how to implement data contracts in your organization. We'll discuss how to get started with your implementation by identifying a strong use case and using it to prove the concept. We'll also look at the minimal data contract implementation you need to support that proof of concept.

Next, we'll build on that and discuss how to migrate the rest of your datasets to data contracts and consider a couple of approaches to doing that. That will lead to more data contracts being created. And that, with the increased distribution of ownership, means we'll need to provide some services to help with the discovery of data contracts, so we'll look at what those services are and why they are needed. Finally, we'll look at what is required to build a mature data contracts-backed data culture.

As with any introduction of a new approach and architecture to an organization, it can feel daunting, but by the end of this chapter, you'll have everything you need to start your journey and progress toward building a truly data-driven organization, backed by data contracts.

In this chapter, we're going to cover the following main topics:

- Getting started with data contracts
- Migrating to data contracts
- Discovering data contracts
- Building a mature data contracts-backed data culture

Getting started with data contracts

In this section, we're going to look at exactly how to get started with implementing data contracts in your organization. We'll learn how to identify a use case, prove the concept, and build the minimum required tooling.

The first step is to decide on your key objective(s) for implementing data contracts in your organization. What are the problems you want to solve first, and why are they important to the business?

This could be improving the dependability and performance of your data pipelines, maybe because you are seeing that users are losing trust in the data they are being provided and lack confidence in using it to support their decision-making. Or, it could be you want to make your data more accessible and easier to use in business-critical applications, including machine learning applications, as the development and successful deployment of those applications form an important part of the business goals.

Whatever it is, you need to be clear on your objectives and the problems you want to solve. To start with, you probably want to focus on one or two of these objectives, while keeping in mind a vision for where your organization will be once data contracts have been successfully adopted and the data culture has changed with it.

The next step is to find a use case where deploying data contracts will help with that objective. This will be our **proof of concept** (POC) where, through data contracts, we'll be delivering some value while laying the foundations with our tooling to support further adoption. As well as being a relevant use case, it also needs the right people and resources available to support the POC. This will include the data generators, who will take on the responsibility for the data and make changes to produce data that aligns with the contract, and the data consumers, who know what data they need and the value they can create with that data.

With that in place, we can already start having conversations about the data contracts. The data consumers can start defining what they need, where the interface should be, and the expected requirements. Notice how we're already starting to bring the data generators and data consumers together! See *Chapter 4, Bringing Data Consumers and Generators Closer Together*, for more information on why this is important and how to approach it.

Now we can start thinking about the data contract tooling we need to support this use case. When designing this tooling, we need to ensure it will support the decentralization and assignment of ownership goals of data contracts, as we discussed in *Chapter 2, Introducing Data Contracts*. Data generators must be able to self-serve the tooling, so we're not building in new bottlenecks or reducing their autonomy.

It's best to get the data generators involved with the design of the tooling. This could include those working on the POC and other interested parties around the organization. As well as likely leading to a better outcome, this gives them a sense of ownership over the project and its outcomes. Once the POC has been successfully delivered, these early stakeholders become cheerleaders for data contracts as you roll them out across the business.

We should aim to build the **minimum viable product** (MVP) required to support the POC and deliver it as quickly as possible. We will deliver the minimum functionality we can with regular deliverables to the users, taking their feedback and iterating on it further. Just as with our data products, we will apply a product mindset to the data contracts-backed platform we are creating. We may change our scope of *minimum* and *viable* for these deliverables, but it's still a *product* and still needs to be of the right quality.

There are three parts of this tooling we need in place for any minimal data contract implementation:

- The ability to define a data contract
- The ability to provision an interface for the data for consumers to query
- The ability for generators to write data to that interface

Let's look at each of these in turn in the following sections.

The ability to define a data contract

In this section, we're going to look at *how* to define data contracts, *where* to store them, and *what* to capture in them, and consider how best to make those decisions.

As we discussed in *Chapter 6, What Makes Up a Data Contract*, we have a few options when deciding how and where to define a data contract. When deciding which to use for your organization, it's likely best to choose one that is already well-established and familiar to the data generators.

For example, at GoCardless we define our data contracts in Jsonnet (`https://jsonnet.org`). That's because Jsonnet was already widely used by our engineering teams, as it's how they provision resources and deploy services through our infrastructure platform. There's nothing that makes Jsonnet a better choice for data contracts than anything else, but it was the obvious choice for us and meant the data generators didn't have to learn how to use a new definition language, and we didn't have to implement any new tooling to support that language.

If you don't have any existing tooling that you can build on or align with, then the best option is probably YAML, as we used in *Chapter 8, A Sample Implementation*. It's widely popular, so many users will be familiar with it, and it's both human- and machine-readable, so we can easily build on it as we develop our tooling.

Once we have decided *how* to define data contracts, we next need to decide *where* to store them.

Again, the best place is probably where your data generators already are, or somewhere they would most expect them to be, given what is already available in your organization. For us at GoCardless, that was in the central repository that contained the infrastructure code. It also allowed us to build on all that existing tooling and was by far the quickest way to build our MVP.

If you don't have something to build on, then you have a few options. You could create a code repository to hold the data contracts and build your tooling on that. Or you could allow data contracts to be defined alongside the data generators' code, in their existing repositories. This has the benefit of reinforcing the decentralization and ownership goals, as well as making it easier for data generators to use the contracts in their tests and through their continuous integration systems. However, the implementation can be a lot more difficult, so that's a trade-off you'll need to make.

Now we've decided how and where to define a data contract, we finally need to consider *what* we want to capture in that contract. As we discussed in *Chapter 7, A Contract-Driven Data Architecture*, metadata allows us to provision resources to deploy tooling that supports data. It can also drive our data governance implementation, as discussed in *Chapter 5, Embedding Data Governance*.

This is where you need to balance the need to produce an MVP quickly with your vision for data contracts in the future. To support this POC, you may only need the following defined in your data contract:

- The name of the data contract
- The owner
- The schema, including fields and their types
- The interface where the data will be written to by the data generators and consumed from by the data consumers

However, we know we will want to support the evolution of data contracts, so we should have a version number captured there. We may also have a good idea of how we want to support our data governance implementation, so we could already enforce the categorization of data, for example, whether it contains personal data and/or whether that data is personally identifiable.

Even if you're not planning to build data governance tooling anytime soon, it could still be worthwhile having this categorization as a requirement from the start. It will prevent you from going back to the data generators later and asking them to categorize the data, which is always a difficult ask when they have moved on from the project.

Bringing all this together, you might have a data contract defined as something like the following example:

```
name: Customer
description: A customer of our e-commerce website.
owner: product-team@data-contracts.com
version: 1
warehouse_path: app.customers
fields:
    name:
        type: string
        description: The name of the customer.
        personal_data: true
        anonymization_strategy: hex
    email:
        type: string
        description: The email address of the customer.
        personal_data: true
        anonymization_strategy: email
```

But of course, you can't expect all the decisions you make now to be perfect! Even if they are the best decisions you can make now, things change both internally within your organization and externally, with regulations and other requirements. That's why *the data contract definition itself must be versioned.*

For example, in our Jsonnet definition at GoCardless, our data contracts version is part of the function call to create a new one, as shown in the following code snippet:

```
datacontracts.v1.new({...})
```

If you're using YAML or similar, you could put the version number in the path of the file, in the name of the code repository, or wherever else makes the most sense for you. But it must allow you to make a breaking change to the contract definition without needing to migrate all data contracts and their data at the same time, as that would be very time-consuming and highly risky.

By having the data contract definition itself versioned, we're giving ourselves options in the future to make large changes. If we did so, it would still require a migration plan and we'd still have to work with our data generators and/or consumers. We'll avoid this work if we can, but if not, it's achievable.

The importance of versioning

Versioning has come up a lot in this book! We've spoken about how important it is to version the data contract and the interface (for example, the table in the data warehouse) provided through it. We do that to ensure stability. We prevent any breaking changes from being made to that version of the interface. When a breaking change does need to be made, a new version is created, with a planned migration to that new version (as discussed in *Chapter 6, What Makes Up a Data Contract,* in the *Evolving your data over time* section).

Now we've discussed how the data contract definition itself must also be versioned, and the reasons are the same! We want the definition to be stable so our users can build on data contracts with confidence, without a breaking change to that definition affecting their data or their consumers. But we also need the ability to evolve that definition, and when we do, we'll perform a planned migration to that new version.

That just shows how important this is as a concept, and how any kind of interface being provided to users should be versioned.

Now we can define data contracts, have somewhere to store them, and decide what they should contain, let's look next and how to use them to create an interface for the data.

The ability to provision an interface for the data for consumers to query

Let's look now at how to provide the interface data consumers will query, using the data contract definition we decided on in the previous section.

Typically, this interface will be a table in a data warehouse or lakehouse, such as Snowflake or Google BigQuery, but it could also be a topic on an event streaming platform such as Apache Kafka or Google Pub/Sub. For this MVP, we want to avoid bringing in new platforms of that complexity, so it's likely best to use whatever we already have in place.

As we discussed in *Chapter 7, A Contract-Driven Data Architecture*, we'll be using the data contract to provision the interface. The tooling we build will use the schema defined in the contract to configure the schema for the interface and keep them aligned as the data contract evolves.

We want to allow for *flexibility* in these schemas. We don't want to tell generators they must structure their data in a certain way. Instead, we want them to have the *autonomy* to decide how best to structure the data, so it meets the requirements of the data consumers.

Data generators must have the ability to self-serve the deployment of this interface. We shouldn't introduce a bottleneck on a central team performing the deployment, or even approving it. We trust our data generators to provision the right interface, with the right schema, through the right data contract. The tooling we have in place should prevent any human errors from negatively affecting that deployment.

We may also provide various options for configuring the interface, but this could be something we can cut from the scope of the MVP if it's not essential for the POC. For example, we may like to optimize the provision of access controls. But for now, we can configure that outside of the data contract, through whatever existing method you use to configure your resources.

With the interface provisioned through the data contract, let's finally look at how data generators write to the interface.

The ability of generators to write data to the interface

The final part of the tooling we'll need to support the POC gives the data generators the ability to write data to the interface we provisioned in the previous section.

The easiest way to do this is to write directly to that interface, and if that works for your use case then that is likely what you should do. If you're using a popular warehouse, lakehouse, or event streaming platform, there will be libraries available that make it easy to write to them in whatever programming language your data generators are using.

However, for some use cases, there will be a bit more complexity involved.

Often, we need the data that is made for consumption to be consistent with the source system. But how do we guarantee that is the case when writing to two different systems: the services database and the data consumers' interface?

One of the most popular methods to achieve this is the **transactional outbox pattern**. With this, the service only writes to its database directly. When it does so, as well as updating its internal models, it *also* writes an event to a separate table in the database, known as the *outbox*. At some time later, this event is taken from the outbox and written to our data contracts-backed interface, ready for consumption.

The key feature of the pattern is that these writes all happen within the same database transaction. If the service fails to write the record to its internal models, an event will not be written to the outbox. If the service fails to write to the outbox, the internal models will not be updated. This is how we guarantee consistency.

The following diagram shows the transactional outbox pattern in action:

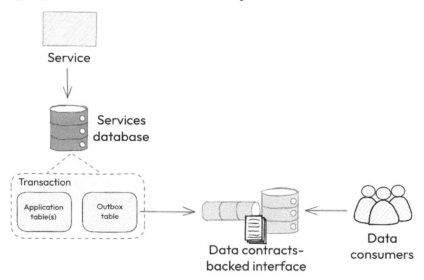

Figure 9.1 – The transactional outbox pattern

If the transactional outbox pattern is already in use in your organization, this is a great method to use to generate events, using the existing tooling and libraries you have.

An alternative might be to build on your **change data capture** (**CDC**) service if you have one. Instead of having the data generators write to the interface from their service, they could maintain a small pipeline that uses the CDC data to populate the interface. The CDC service provides transactional guarantees, but the downside to this approach is software engineers have to learn how to build and maintain these data pipelines and update them as their internal models change. It's better than having another team try to do this without their context, but we're still relying on the internal models of the database for consumption, so I wouldn't recommend this in the long term.

This pattern is shown in the following diagram:

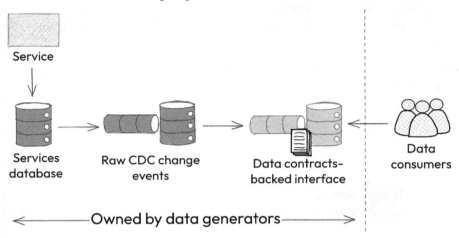

Figure 9.2 – Materialized views on a change data capture service,
with those views owned by the data generators

However, if you can get away without needing this strong data consistency in the datasets for your use case, you can avoid a lot of complexity and improve performance. So, it is always worth questioning how important the transactional guarantee is for each use case you have.

We'll cover all of this in more detail and introduce other useful patterns in *Chapter 10, Data Contracts in Practice*, in the *Data contracts publishing patterns* section.

We now have the three parts of the tooling we need for our MVP:

- The ability to define a data contract
- The ability to provision an interface for the data for consumers to query
- The ability for generators to write data to that interface

This tooling and how it works together is shown in the following diagram, with the data consumers consuming data from our interface:

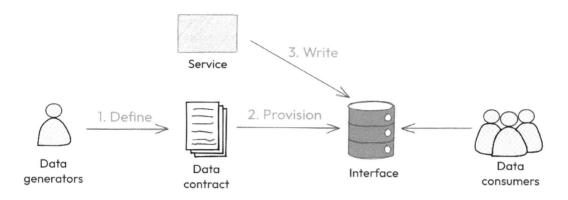

Figure 9.3 – The minimum viable data contract tooling

We now have everything in place to support the POC and prove the value of data contracts. Following on from the success of this, we'll start migrating the rest of our data assets to data contracts. Let's look at how to do that next.

Migrating to data contracts

Now we've proved the concept of data contracts and started delivering some value, let's look at how to migrate the rest of our data assets to data contracts.

We'll need to come up with a migration plan that balances the need to complete this migration in a reasonable amount of time, so we can decommission our legacy platform and tools, against the needs of product teams to deliver against their existing roadmaps and commitments.

Unfortunately, there is no perfect way to do this, and the approach you take will highly depend on your organization and its objectives.

One good approach is to ask your key data consumers (typically data/analytics engineers and data scientists) to work together and prioritize the datasets most critical to them. This could take the form of a working group, where a few people from each team will work together on this exercise. There's likely to be a lot of overlap, as those teams and other data consumers will care most about the same core data models that are at the heart of your business.

With this, we can go to the data generators and make the case for a data contract to be provided for this data. As we discussed in *Chapter 3, How To Get Adoption In Your Organization*, we will need to clearly articulate the value this data provides you and your end users, and use the company-wide goals to help incentivize the data generators to take on this work.

Another approach might be to set a deadline for the migration. This could be a date when you need to decommission your existing architecture, or something more arbitrary. The risk with this approach is that the data generators may not buy into the objectives as much and instead look for the quickest way to hit the deadline. If this happens, we haven't done much to bring the data generators and data consumers together – we've just changed the tooling used to move data around.

Whichever approach we take, it can sometimes be difficult to assign ownership to datasets, particularly those that have shared ownership over teams and groups. At this stage, it can be simplest to assign ownership of the data to the team that owns the service that generated the data. That should roll out to the right group and domain. As we increase adoption and maturity, those groups can change the ownership within the domain as needed.

Throughout the migration, we should regularly measure its progress and communicate its impact. Simple measures such as the adoption rate are useful for keeping track of progress. Other measures that help more on the impact might include the amount of data incidents you have, which we'd expect to decrease with more adoption as the quality and stability of the data improves. We might also expect the costs associated with your ETL to decrease.

These can be communicated regularly to the business using newsletters and other internal communications. We may have different methods to communicate to different audiences, tailoring the message to them. They could include recognition of those teams who have successfully migrated to data contracts, celebrating the impact of that change.

As we progress with the migration, we'll need to keep iterating on the tooling, providing more self-serve capabilities that meet the needs of our growing number of data generators. This might include governance tooling that automates the handling of data, tools that automate backups, or tools that help with the migration of data as schemas evolve.

It may also include some centralized services. For example, we may want to build a data catalog, to make it easier for data consumers to find data backed by a data contract. We might also need some data lineage capabilities. As we migrate more datasets to data contracts and move ownership to the data owners, the amount of data owners grows. Data lineage allows us to more easily find the owners of the datasets that we depend on, whoever they may be. We'll discuss the importance of data catalogs and data lineage later in this chapter, in the *Discovering data contracts* section.

Now is probably a good time to make the case for a data infrastructure team, dedicated to building and supporting this data contract tooling. We discussed this team and how to make a case for it in *Chapter 7, A Contract-Driven Data Architecture*.

With this investment and continuous iteration, we are building out our data contract tooling and supporting services. We'll now have an architecture similar to the one shown in the following diagram:

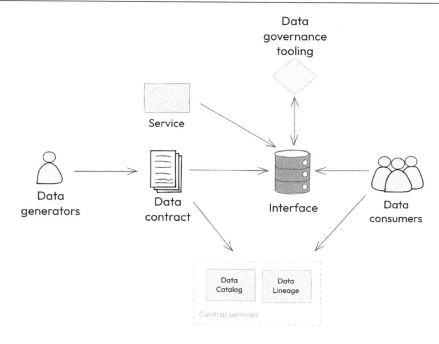

Figure 9.4 – Building out our data contract tooling and supporting services

We're now well on the way with our migration to data contracts. But, with this increase in data contracts and the distribution of ownership, we'll need to provide some support to data consumers that helps them discover them. Let's look at that next.

Discovering data contracts

As the amount of data contracts increase and we successfully shift ownership of those left to the data generators, the ownership of data increases. That will make it more difficult for data consumers to know where the data is, how to access it, and who owns it.

There are two related tools that can help us with this problem: a data catalog, and data lineage. In this section, we'll introduce each of these tools in turn and explain why they are important when implementing data contracts in your organization.

We'll cover the following topics in this section:

- What is a data catalog?
- Why are data catalogs important for discovering data contracts?
- What is data lineage?
- Why is data lineage important for data contracts?

What is a data catalog?

Before discussing how data catalogs help us discover data products built with data contracts, let's first explain what a data catalog is.

A **data catalog** is an inventory of our organization's available data. It is centralized, providing a single place to search for and discover data products no matter where they reside, who owns them, or what domain they belong to. It aims to improve productivity by allowing any potential consumer of data to autonomously find and access that data through a self-serve interface.

This is an important part of supporting a data-driven organization. By improving the discovery and accessibility of the data, users can spend more time creating value from that data by using it to support their decision making and embedding that data into their applications.

The data catalog provides users with the context they need to make effective use of the data products they describe. This may include the following attributes:

- The owner of the data product
- Documentation on what the data product contains and how to use it
- The format and schema of the data
- The expectations of the data, including its criticality, support levels, and any **service-level objectives (SLOs)**
- Where the data is stored, and how to address it through the correct interface
- Access controls, and how to request access
- Compliance requirements and data usage policies

In short, the data catalog should contain everything a data consumer needs to know so they can use the data product *with confidence*.

Organizations have benefitted from the use of data catalogs for many years. They are particularly important when promoting the use of decentralized data products, as we are with data contracts. Let's discuss why that is in the next section.

Why are data catalogs important for discovering data contracts?

Now we understand what data catalogs are and the features they provide, let's look at why they are such an important tool to support your data contract implementation.

As we've been discussing throughout this book, with data contracts we're moving to a decentralized data architecture, where data is owned by the data generators within a particular domain. That data is then made available to consumers through an interface, which, as we discussed in *Chapter 7, A*

Contract-Driven Data Architecture, will be isolated to help promote ownership and limit the impact of any issues.

For example, that interface could be a table in your data lakehouse that resides within an area (for example, a project or database) for that domain. There may be many different domains, each with its own area in the data lakehouse. While modern data lakehouses allow us to query across different areas without penalty, we need a way to discover those data products and find out how to address them.

The data catalog solves this problem. It's a centralized inventory of all the data products in our organization, across all domains, and from all data generators. It's what allows our data to be *isolated*, but not *siloed*, and promotes a federalized data architecture where access to data can be self-served.

We can use the data contract to populate the data catalog, creating an entry for each data product. Every attribute we want to populate about that data product, including all those we listed in the previous section, is defined in the data contract, which remains the source of truth. The data generators remain responsible for keeping the data contract, including those attributes, up to date.

Another tool that's increasingly important to support the implementation of data contracts is a data lineage tool. Let's look at what that is, and why it's important, next.

What is data lineage?

Let's start by exploring what data lineage is, before looking at why it is increasingly important in a data contract-driven architecture.

Data lineage tracks the relationships between data products, both upstream and downstream, including their use in data applications such as reporting tools or ML models. From any given point, it allows you to see the origin of the data, how it has been processed and transformed, and where the data product is used.

This traceability of data as it moves around your organization allows you to see how and where the data is being used. This can be useful for impact analysis, for example, seeing who would be affected by evolving a schema, or who is affected by an ongoing incident. It can also be used to meet compliance and regulatory requirements around the access and processing of data, which can help explain how a decision was made, for example, by an ML model.

Consumers of data can use the lineage information to understand how the data they are using was generated. The transparency and visibility help the user trust the data they are using, giving them the *confidence* to use that data to support their decision-making or integrate it into their applications.

Data engineering teams are often already heavy users of data lineage. They use it to understand their pipelines and identify any performance bottlenecks that can be optimized. By looking at the patterns in tables of queries by downstream consumers, they can consider refactors that reduce costs.

Lineage is also useful for troubleshooting issues with their data pipelines, particularly as the complexity of those will have grown as they attempt to ingest and transform raw data from many different sources.

With data contracts, we want to remove a lot of that complexity by encouraging the creation of quality data products. However, that doesn't lessen the importance of lineage – in fact, it increases it, as we'll discuss next.

Why is data lineage important for data contracts?

With that understanding of data lineage, let's look at why it becomes even more important when implementing data contracts.

As mentioned in the *Discovering data contracts* section previously, with data contracts we're moving to a decentralized architecture, where data is owned by the data generators within a particular domain.

This means that the ownership of the data grows. Previously, you might have assumed that for any data question you have, for example, on the use of that data, how to get access, and whether it is performing as expected, you would have asked a centralized data team. Now, they are not likely to be the owners of that data and won't have the answers you need. Instead, that owner will be a data generator in the business domain that owns that data.

Not only that, but the ownership may change at each step in the supply chain of data products that ultimately lead to the data product you are consuming from, as data is enriched both within that domain and as it passes to other domains.

Data lineage solves this problem by making it easy to see what data you depend on at every step and the owner of that step. It gives you the confidence to use that data, knowing you can find out who to contact if you need more context on the data or in the event of an issue.

There are many data lineage tools available, both paid and open source. They often include data catalog functionality, so you may be able to find one tool that satisfies both these requirements and supports your implementation of data contracts.

With the data catalog and data lineage implemented, we have everything we need implemented in our tooling. But that's only one part of our objective. We also wanted to change the data culture. So now let's look at what else we need to put in place to build a mature data contracts-backed data culture.

Building a mature data contracts-backed data culture

In this section, we'll look at what to build as your data culture matures through the adoption of data contracts.

Data contracts should now be an explicit part of your organization's strategy and architecture. You expect all useful data to be provided through data contracts, providing the interface and all the tooling to support that data.

We'll have formalized the concept of **data products** within the organization, hiring data product managers to take on the responsibility of creating great data products that meet the requirements of the data consumers. As we discussed in *Chapter 3, How To Get Adoption In Your Organization*, by adopting a data product mindset and creating data products for the rest of your organization to consume, you increase the amount of accessible data you have available to drive business outcomes. With better data quality from the source, we reduce the time to insight and action, as well as reducing costs.

We may also want to consider the organizational structure that supports these data products. We can get quite far on our journey toward maturity by asking software engineers to build and support these data products. However, when you start having many of these data products in each group or domain, it may be better to put together a specialist data engineering team to build and support them.

Being embedded in that group, the data engineers will gain a good understanding of the domain and the data that describes it. They will see how it has changed over time and have visibility of how it might change in the future. Their expertise and focus will allow them to perform tasks such as **data domain modeling**, leading to data products that are better optimized for the data lakehouse they reside in, reducing the costs of consumption by users.

How easy this is to achieve depends on your existing organizational structure. Many organizations have experience building these cross-functional teams, with specialists such as designers, quality assurance, or site reliability engineers embedded within teams. These specialists benefit from gaining a deeper understanding of the group's domain and the problems they have, and use their expertise to solve those problems quickly and effectively.

If this is new to your organization, it may be more difficult to make the case for cross-functional teams, but there are many resources available to help build that case. Some are listed at the end of this chapter, under the *Further reading* section.

We also want to have a mature data governance process, with the policies set centrally and the responsibility embedded locally and assigned to the data generators. But this shouldn't be much of a burden for them, as we have automated much of this with the tooling we described in *Chapter 5, Embedding Data Governance*. The data generators do not need to be experts in data regulations and best practices. They just need to categorize the data, and the tooling takes care of the rest.

With all this in place, we're well-placed to become a truly data-driven organization. Through data contracts, we have an agreed *interface* between the generators of data and its consumers. We've set the *expectations* around that data, defined how it should be *governed*, and facilitated the *explicit* generation of data that meets the business requirements. We've delivered data contracts as per the four principles we introduced back in *Chapter 2, Introducing Data Contracts*.

Through our adoption of data contracts, we have created the data culture we wanted, where data is supplied through data products that meet user requirements. These products are accessible to and useful for any data consumer, who can trust the data and build on it with *confidence*.

Summary

In this chapter, we've shown how to adopt data contracts in your organization. We discussed how to get started by identifying a suitable use case to prove the concept and supported that with a **minimum viable product (MVP)** of our data tooling.

Once we've proved the value of data contracts, we can start migrating the rest of our datasets over, so we next looked at how to approach that migration. As that progresses, we'll not only have more data contracts, we'll also have increased the distribution of ownership. So, we looked next at how to ensure they remain discoverable and accessible through the implementation of a data catalog and data lineage.

Finally, we developed this further by showing how to build a mature, data contracts-backed data culture that delivers on our objective to become a truly data-driven organization.

In the next chapter, we'll close the book by looking at working with data contracts in practice on a day-to-day level.

Further reading

For more information on the topics covered in this chapter, please see the following resources:

- *What is a Proof of Concept (PoC) in Software Development?* By Piotr Szczechowiak: `https://www.netguru.com/blog/proof-of-concept-in-software-development`

- *Minimum Viable Product - What is a MVP and why is it important*: `https://www.productplan.com/glossary/minimum-viable-product/`

- *How to Get Started with Data Mesh: Strategy and Execution* by Zhamak Dehghani: `https://www.starburst.io/resources/how-to-get-started-with-data-mesh-strategy-and-execution/`

- *Data Catalogs Will Change Data Culture Within Your Company* by Madison Schott: `https://blog.devgenius.io/data-catalogs-will-change-data-culture-within-your-company-49253d72a72`

- *Your Data Catalog Shouldn't Be Just One More UI* by Mahdi Karabiben: `https://towardsdatascience.com/your-data-catalog-shouldnt-be-just-one-more-ui-e6bffb793cf1`

- *Data catalog ROI – A Primer* by Louise de Leyritz: `https://medium.com/castor-app/data-catalog-roi-a-primer-a57d42d054cf`

- *What is Data Lineage and How Can It Ensure Data Quality?* by Michael Bogan: `https://levelup.gitconnected.com/what-is-data-lineage-and-how-can-it-ensure-data-quality-9a15b3c5b48b`

- *Creating a Transparent Data Environment with Data Lineage* by Madison Schott: `https://towardsdatascience.com/creating-a-transparent-data-environment-with-data-lineage-12e449597f6`

- Skelton, M and Pais, M. (2019). *Team Topologies*. IT Revolution Press.

- *What Are Cross Functional Teams?* By Christine Organ and Cassie Bottorff: `https://www.forbes.com/advisor/business/cross-functional-teams/`

- *How to Build a Cross-Functional Team*: `https://www.atlassian.com/work-management/project-collaboration/cross-functional-teams`

- *A Brief Introduction to Domain Modeling* by Oleg Chursin: `https://olegchursin.medium.com/a-brief-introduction-to-domain-modeling-862a30b38353`

10

Data Contracts in Practice

In this final chapter, we'll look at working with data contracts in practice, on a day-to-day basis. We'll start by looking at how to design a data contract, breaking that down into four easy steps that, through strong collaboration between the data generators and the data consumers, will lead to a data contract being deployed to production.

Next, we'll look at enforcing and monitoring these data contracts. This includes the data contract definition itself, the quality of the data, and the performance and dependability of the data. We'll provide solutions that guarantee the quality of the data through the data contract.

Finally, we'll look at how best to publish data to a data contract. This can be more complex than it sounds as there are a few things you need to consider when publishing the data if it needs a high level of consistency between the source system and the data contract. We'll describe a few implementation patterns that can be used to publish the data and discuss their benefits and drawbacks.

By the end of this chapter, you'll have everything you need to drive data quality with data contracts.

In this chapter, we're going to cover the following main topics:

- Designing a data contract
- Monitoring and enforcing data contracts
- Data contract publishing patterns

Designing a data contract

We'll start by looking at how to design a data contract. This can be broken down into four steps:

1. Identifying the purpose.
2. Considering the trade-offs.
3. Defining the data contract.
4. Deploying the data contract.

However, designing a data contract is an iterative process, and you may need to revisit and refine these steps as more information is gathered through discussions between the data generators and data consumers.

With that in mind, let's look at each step in turn.

Identifying the purpose

The first step is to identify the purpose of this data product for which you are defining a data contract. Who is this data for, and how will they use it? What problems will it solve? What business value will it drive?

Answering these questions will naturally start a discussion between the data generators and the data consumers, and as we've been discussing throughout this book, bringing these groups of people together is one of the key objectives of data contracts. See *Chapter 4, Bringing Data Consumers and Generators Closer Together*, for more on this.

Through these discussions, the data generators can collect the requirements of the data consumers. Those requirements could include the following:

- The data they need
- What structure it needs to be in
- The interface they need to consume from and its availability
- How timely the data needs to be
- Whether we can accept incomplete data, and if so, how much

However, these requirements may not necessarily be something the data generators can meet. There will be various trade-offs they will need to consider before committing to this data contract. We'll look at those next.

Considering the trade-offs

The data generators will need to consider various trade-offs, constraints, and limitations before they can commit to meeting the data contract.

Some of these could impact how the data is structured. For example, it may be quite expensive to generate events that contain all the fields being requested. That expense could be the cost of compute or other resources or could be the performance impact it has on the service generating the data.

They may also not be able to meet some of the performance requirements requested by the data consumers. For example, it could be the existing methods to publish data to the requested interface are too slow to meet that requirement.

This is why *the data generator must own the data contract*. Only they have the full context of their service and the data to make these decisions. They will be the ones generating and publishing the data and supporting it in the long term, so they need to be comfortable with the responsibilities they are signing up for.

After this, there will be more discussions between the data generators and the data consumers around the specifics of the requirements. Maybe the scope will change, or the consumers will decide they can still deliver most of the value with less performant data. Or maybe the value of the data application means extra work can be prioritized by the data generators and/or teams that support the data contract's implementation.

All of this should be captured in a document somewhere. This could be in a standard project document or a **request for comment** (RFC) document that's already in use in your organization, or you may have something specific for data contract discussions. This document supports these discussions and allows you to review the decisions that have been taken.

Eventually, the data generators and the data consumers will come to an *agreement* and will be ready to start defining the data contract itself. We'll discuss what that will look like next.

Defining the data contract

At this stage, we can start to get into the specifics of the data contract, which forms the agreement between the data generators and the data consumers. This will include the schema of the data and all the fields. They will have some documentation associated with them to make it clear to everyone exactly what they are, and their data types will have been defined.

We may also want to start defining some data quality checks if we have that functionality in our data contracts and can measure and enforce them once it has been deployed. For example, we might specify a valid range for a numeric value, that a string matches a known format (for example, an email address), and so on. We'll discuss how to monitor and enforce these data quality checks later in this chapter, in the *Monitoring and enforcing data contracts* section.

The data contract should also have SLOs defined. These should be at a level the data generator feels comfortable meeting and should be no higher than the minimum required by the data consumers. Increasing the performance and dependability of data is costly, and that cost increases exponentially as the target level increases. Going beyond what is required is a waste of money and effort.

Finally, we will want to categorize the data to comply with our data governance policies, particularly if they impact the use of the data downstream. See *Chapter 5, Embedding Data Governance*, for more information on why this is important and how we can use this categorization to automate data governance.

With all this agreed, we're ready to deploy the data contract.

Deploying the data contract

Now that we have an agreement between the data generators and the data consumers and have defined the data contract, we're ready to deploy it to production. Exactly how you do that depends on how you've implemented data contracts, but if you've been following the guidance in this book, you will probably merge to a Git repository, after which the interface and any services that support the data contract will be provisioned and deployed. See *Chapter 7, A Contract-Driven Data Architecture*, for more information on how to build that.

Once deployed, the data generator can start writing data to the interface, which can then be consumed by the data consumer. Writing the data can sometimes be more complex than it sounds. We'll discuss why that is and offer some patterns to help you with this later in this chapter, in the *Data contracts publishing patterns* section.

Other tasks may also be required. For example, often, the data consumer will need access to historical data, which the data generator will need to backfill into this interface. Some monitoring may also need to be set up on the data, including the data quality checks. We'll discuss that in more detail shortly in the *Monitoring and enforcing data contracts* section.

Following this, we should now have a data contract providing an interface to a quality data product! It's ready to be consumed by data consumers, who can use it to deliver some business value.

But to ensure that the data being published continues to match the contract, we'll want to implement some monitoring and enforcement. We'll look at this in detail in the next section.

Monitoring and enforcing data contracts

In this section, we'll look at how to monitor and enforce our data contracts. This is important, as one of the four principles we looked at in *Chapter 2, Introducing Data Contracts*, is setting expectations. There's little point in setting these expectations if we cannot prove we're meeting them. It's that proof that gives data consumers the *confidence* to build on this data.

There are three areas where we can add some monitoring and/or enforcement:

- The data contract's definition
- The quality of the data
- The performance and dependability of the data

Let's look at each of these in turn.

The data contract's definition

Data contracts are written by humans and, as such, are susceptible to human error. They are also intended to be self-served, without requiring a central review, as that slows teams down and reduces their autonomy. Therefore, we will want to add some automated checks to ensure the data contract itself is valid before any mistakes are deployed to production.

The first set of enforcement we'll need will ensure certain metadata fields are present in the data contract. This will likely include checking it has a valid version number, an owner, some documentation, and so on.

Then, for each field, we will want to ensure it has, at a minimum, a name, a type, and a description. If we've also embedded data governance (as discussed in *Chapter 5, Embedding Data Governance*) we may want to check that the field has been categorized, and, if it contains personal data, has an anonymization strategy defined.

As we continue to invest in data contracts, we will be adding more to our data contract definition. For example, we might allow data generators to define SLOs in the data contract, and we could add checks to ensure they are set correctly with a valid measure.

Whatever definition language we've chosen to define our data contract in (for example, Avro, JSON, or YAML), it should be easy to write some code that performs those validations, as we did in *Chapter 8, A Sample Implementation*. Alternatively, we can make use of tools such as CUE (`https://cuelang. org/`) to validate YAML and JSON-based data contracts by simply defining those using its concise validation syntax and running its command-line tool.

We will also need some checks to ensure schema evolution is managed correctly. We'll want to prevent breaking changes, such as the removal of a required field, from being applied to an existing data contract in production as that could impact data consumers or, in the worst case, lead to data loss.

Again, we could write code to implement this ourselves, but it's probably easiest to rely on a schema registry to perform those checks for you, particularly as we will likely need one anyway to make the schemas available to different tools and services. We also showed this in *Chapter 8, A Sample Implementation*, in the *Managing schema evolution* section.

To prevent invalid contracts from being released to production, we will run these checks as part of our continuous integration pipelines. These will be triggered when a data generator pushes their commit to their code repository and will only allow that commit to be released to production if each of the checks is successful.

Once the data contract has been deployed to production, we can publish data through it. Next, we'll look at how to monitor that data and enforce the data contract.

The quality of the data

In this section, we'll look at how to enforce and monitor the *quality* of our data. By quality, we mean *does the data itself match our expectations?* We'll cover the following topics:

- The two types of data quality issues
- Where to implement data quality checks

The two types of data quality issues

There are two types of data quality issues we can enforce and/or monitor: those we predicted and tested for in advance, and those we didn't.

The issues we predicted and tested in advance include everything we define in our schemas. For example, we know that if a number suddenly became a string, that would break any mathematical functions being run on that number downstream. So, we make use of schemas to protect us from that issue. They also include any tests on the data we perform, such as ensuring a number is within a certain range. Depending on where these tests are implemented, they can prevent the issue from affecting downstream data consumers directly and only need to be resolved in the affected system.

However, in complex systems, we'll never predict every possible failure – nor should we assume we could. There is a range of issues that will occur that we didn't think of implementing checks for in advance. Each of these issues may rarely happen, but there are many of them, so we should expect them to occur regularly. Examples might include a distribution anomaly or even a code change that prevented our predicted tests from running, allowing invalid data to be published.

The best defense against these unpredictable data quality issues is to try to build applications that are resilient to failure. For example, your application may not expect a particular record to contain a timestamp in the future and that may cause an exception, but that exception doesn't have to prevent the valid records that come after it from being processed. Those invalid records could be written to a **dead letter queue**, which takes them out of the service and stores them somewhere to aid with debugging and allows us to replay that data once the issue has been resolved.

We can also make use of data observability tools to detect these issues. They use techniques such as data profiling and anomaly detection to look at how recent data compares to previous records and can alert us if they identify data that appears to be unexpected.

These issues are usually detected *after* the data has been published from the source system, so they may impact downstream consumers directly until the issue is resolved. However, by making use of observability tools, we can at least ensure they are detected quickly and that the data generator is alerted as soon as possible – ideally before the downstream consumers notice.

Now, let's look at where we can implement both types of data quality checks while using data contracts.

Where to implement data quality checks

There are three places we can implement monitoring and enforce data quality to catch data quality issues:

- At publishing time
- In the infrastructure
- After publishing

The first two have the benefit that any issues identified can be contained at the source system. The data does not get written to the interface and therefore does not directly impact every data consumer. This limits the scope of the incident and reduces the time to resolution.

Identifying issues after the data has been published means the data may have already been consumed by data consumers, who may or may not have been resilient to that issue. Furthermore, once the issue has been resolved, the data may have to be republished to the consumers so that they can correct the data in their applications, and the owners of those applications may need to take some manual action.

The following diagram shows the three different places we can monitor and enforce data quality:

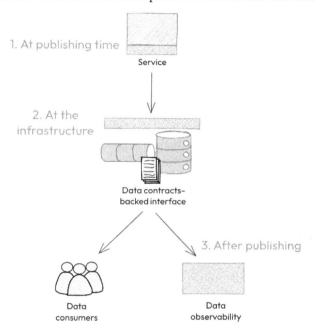

Figure 10.1 – Implementing data quality checks at publishing
time, in the infrastructure, and after publishing

Implementing these checks at the infrastructure level is often the easiest to do. As part of our data contracts implementation, we are creating resources to support the generation of data and providing the interface to be used to consume the data. These resources typically have support to define a schema and will not allow data to be written to it if it does not match that schema.

For example, by having a table in the data warehouse driven by a data contract, as we showed in *Chapter 8, A Sample Implementation*, we know that the schema will always match the one defined in the contract. A data generator cannot write data to that interface that doesn't match the schema and they will get an error if they try to do so. A data consumer will know they can rely on this schema and that there won't be a breaking change on it unless a new version of the contract is deployed.

Aside from tables in data warehouses and lakehouses, many event streaming platforms also support schemas, including Apache Kafka and Google Cloud Pub/Sub, and work in much the same way.

However, these schemas only check that the basic types are correct. We also want to check that the data itself is as expected – for example, the numbers are within a certain range, or the string matches a certain format, such as an email address or country code.

We can implement these checks at publishing time by providing libraries for our data generators to use. These libraries can look up the quality checks defined in the data contract, perhaps from a schema registry, and run those tests on each record. If the tests fail, the data will not be written downstream and the owner of the service – the data generator – will receive an alert.

We can provide custom libraries for our data consumers that implement the checks defined in the data, or we can use something such as JSON Schema and take advantage of existing libraries. This is what we did in *Chapter 8, A Sample Implementation*, in the *Creating libraries for data generators* section.

If we can't enforce these checks at publishing time, an alternative is to monitor the data's quality by running these checks after publishing. This can be implemented using tools such as Great Expectations (`https://greatexpectations.io`) and Soda (`https://www.soda.io`). This is likely the only option you will have when validating data that's been generated or transformed as part of a batch pipeline, such as when using something like dbt (`https://www.getdbt.com/`). However, as mentioned previously, this does mean the data may have already been consumed and that the impact of the issue could be greater.

After publishing is also where we typically deploy data observability tools to catch those issues we hadn't predicted would occur. This is because they often query the interface directly and may need to query large amounts of historical data to detect any anomalies.

By implementing data quality checks across these three places, we can catch data quality issues quickly and limit their impact.

Now, let's look at the final area we want to monitor and enforce with data contracts – the performance and dependability of the data.

The performance and dependability of the data

The final area of monitoring is around the performance and dependability of the data being published through our data contract.

As we discussed in *Chapter 2, Introducing Data Contracts*, these are key expectations a data consumer needs to know if they are to build on this data with confidence. For example, depending on their use case, they may need to know if the data is going to be available to be queried within 1 second, 10 minutes, or 1 hour. With that expectation set, they can decide if it is suitable for their use case and, if so, set expectations for *their* users based on those timings.

These **service-level objectives (SLOs)** can be defined in the data contract. From there, they can be used as part of the documentation of the data contract, so that the data consumers are aware of it, and automate the process of collecting and reporting these metrics.

For example, if we were using a YAML-based data contract, we could add the following fields to it to allow the data generator to define the SLOs for this data product:

```
slos:
  completeness_percent: 100
  timeliness_mins: 60
  availability_percent: 95
```

Automating the process of collecting and reporting these SLOs depends on the resources you are using to support your data contract's implementation and the monitoring stack you use. But to illustrate how this could be done, we will walk through an example while using Google Cloud Pub/Sub, where, through data contracts and the tooling we provide, we can establish a simple design pattern that makes use of these attributes to automate the collection of our timeliness SLO.

Every event or *message* you send through a Pub/Sub topic is annotated with a few fields by the Pub/Sub servers when it is accepted. One of those is `publishTime`, which is the time at which the message was published to the server. Pub/Sub messages can also be annotated with a set of custom attributes, set by the data-generating service.

Let's say that for data generators to make use of this automation, they must populate a `generationTime` attribute on their Pub/Sub message, which is the time the event was generated in their source system.

Expressed as JSON, our Pub/Sub messages now have the following schema, where `data` is the message itself:

```
{
  "data": string,
  "attributes": {
    generationTime: timestamp,
  },
  "publishTime": timestamp,
}
```

The timeliness of the message is simply `publishTime` subtracted from `generationTime`. This measurement will grow if there is a delay in publishing the message, maybe due to a backlog of events that the service needs to process or an incident that prevented it from writing to Pub/Sub for some time.

We can collect this measurement by implementing a simple monitoring system that runs that calculation in near real time, perhaps on a sample of the data. It could make this measure available to an existing monitoring stack, or it could be responsible for sending an alert to the data generator when that measure breaches the SLO defined in the data contract.

The following diagram shows how we've automated the measurement of this performance-related SLO:

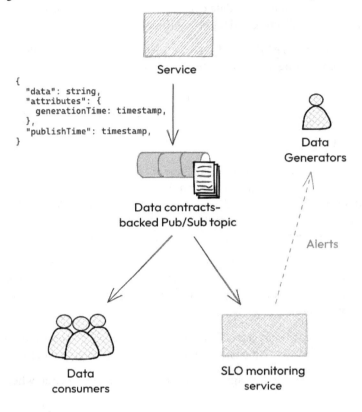

```
{
  "data": string,
  "attributes": {
    generationTime: timestamp,
  },
  "publishTime": timestamp,
}
```

Figure 10.2 – Automating the measurement of the timeliness SLO

This monitoring service could be extended to measure other performance and dependability SLOs, including the completeness and availability of our data, and can do so for any data backed by a data contract.

We now have a well-designed data contract that we can use to monitor and enforce our data governance policies, data quality, and performance and dependability. Next, we'll explore the various patterns a data generator can use to publish their data to the data contract.

Data contract publishing patterns

Data generators need to be able to publish their data easily and reliably to the interface they are providing to their data consumers, which will typically be a table in a data warehouse or lakehouse, such as Snowflake or Google BigQuery, or a topic in an event streaming platform such as Apache Kafka or Google Pub/Sub.

In this section, we'll look at the different patterns they can use to publish their data to these systems, and the pros and cons of each.

Perhaps the key consideration you need to make is whether you need a **transactional guarantee** between the source system and the interface you're providing to the data consumer. It's what ensures *consistency* between the data in our service and the data used by our data consumers.

Consider the scenario where you have a user of the system taking some action that results in a new record being written to the services database – for example, placing an order. Writing to that database is a *single unit of work*. It will either succeed or fail. Whatever the outcome, your data store will correctly reflect the result of that action. This is shown in the following diagram:

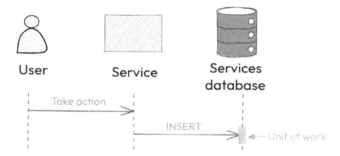

Figure 10.3 – The single unit of work when writing to the database

Now, we want to publish an event that describes that action and makes it available to our consumers through our data contract-backed interface. This becomes a *second unit of work*. To guarantee data consistency, we need these two units of work to be atomic: if one succeeds, the other must succeed. If one fails, the other must also fail.

If you picture how you'd write this in code, you might implement the following steps:

1. Write to the systems database.
2. If successful, write to the data contracts-backed interface.

If we can't write to the systems database, we won't publish to the interface, so that's fine. But what about if we can, but, as illustrated in the following diagram, we can't publish to the interface? This could be because the interface is unavailable, or the service/server crashes in between the two units of work:

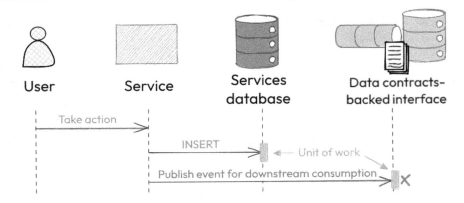

Figure 10.4 – Introducing a second unit of work when writing to the
database and the data contracts-backed interface

To ensure consistency between both data stores, you'd need to be able to prevent that change from being committed to the systems database, restoring it to the previous state. And we can't simply do that as a third unit of work as we're still at risk of breaking the consistency if the service/server crashes. Furthermore, the record may have been updated in the meantime, so we'd potentially lose that update.

This is where we need to implement a transaction guarantee, ensuring data consistency across both units of work.

There are a few patterns to solve this, and they work in the same way. First, you modify only one of these data stores at a time, as a single unit of work. Then, later, that update is applied to the second data store. That second data store is then *eventually consistent* with the first.

We'll cover two of the most popular patterns for implementing transactional guarantees: the *transactional outbox* and the *listen-to-yourself* patterns. However, if you can get away without needing this strong data consistency in the datasets for your use case, you can avoid a lot of complexity and improve performance. So, it is always worth challenging how important this is for each use case you have.

We'll cover the following publishing patterns in turn:

- Writing directly to the interface
- Materialized views on **change data capture** (**CDC**)
- The transactional outbox pattern
- The listen-to-yourself pattern

Writing directly to the interface

The simplest method is, of course, to write directly to the interface itself. If you're using a popular warehouse, lakehouse, or event streaming platform, libraries will be available that make it easy to write to them in whatever programming language your data generators are using.

This simplicity is evident when we draw the implementation, as in the following diagram:

Figure 10.5 – Writing directly to the data contracts-backed interface

However, there are some limitations to this approach, which could make it unsuitable for your use case.

One may be the performance of these writes. Data warehouses and lakehouses tend to be relatively slow at writing single records. If you are storing each record in response to a user action, and that user is waiting for a response stating that the record has been written, it will likely be too slow.

However, they are more optimized for loading large batches of records. So, if you're writing many records as part of a batch process happening asynchronously to the user's interaction, that performance is likely to be good enough.

For streaming platforms, the performance varies but tends to be very good. For example, a well-tuned Apache Kafka setup is reported to be capable of processing ~600 MB/s under benchmarking conditions (`https://developer.confluent.io/learn/kafka-performance/`), which could be fast enough for your use case, even if the user is waiting on a response.

A bigger limitation is that we haven't provided a pattern for handling transactional guarantees. This might be fine, and if it is and you're happy with the performance of the writes, then this is the approach you should use. If not, you'll need a more complex pattern.

We'll look at one of those next, which is implemented on a CDC service.

Materialized views on CDC

CDC services capture the changes that are made to the tables in a transactional database (that is, the `INSERT`, `UPDATE`, and `DELETE` statements ran against the database) and generate events detailing those changes. They can then be used later to recreate the structure and the data in a different database – for example, a data warehouse.

We've discussed CDC a few times already in this book, starting back in *Chapter 1, A Brief History of Data Platforms*. Back then, we spoke about how we wanted to move away from consuming CDC and similar ELT approaches since we're building on the internal models of the upstream service, rather than data that has been explicitly *built for consumption.*

That is still the case! But there is a pattern where you can build on CDC and still provide an interface for data consumers, and that is by having *the data generators maintain a transformed or materialized view of the data on top of the CDC data* – not the data engineers or another data consumer. This pattern is shown in the following diagram:

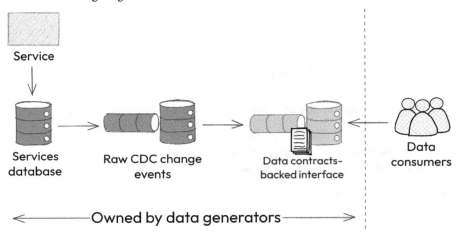

Figure 10.6 – Materialized views on a change data capture service,
with those views owned by the data generators

Let's see what this looks like and consider the benefits and limitations of this approach.

First, we'll need a CDC service in place, which if you don't already have can be quite a complex system to manage. As this CDC service is capturing all the events at the database layer, it takes care of the transactional guarantees some of our use cases might need. Only changes that have been successfully written to the database will be propagated downstream. If that propagation is dependable, we'll have our data consistency.

Most modern CDC implementations have a relatively small impact on the source database's performance. Often, they consume from the replication log, so when all is working well, they add a similar load to adding another database replica. If the CDC service has a problem, it could cause a backlog of events on the database, which, if it becomes too large, could impact the upstream database, so we should ensure it is well-supported and incidents are resolved quickly.

Next, we'll need to provide a way for data generators to transform or materialize the raw CDC change events so that they match the data contract they agreed upon with their consumers, and meet their requirements for dependable and quality data.

If that interface is in a data warehouse, we may need to introduce a tool such as dbt (`https://www.getdbt.com/`) to the organization or, if used already, to our data generators, who in many organizations could be software engineers. Or if it is in an event streaming platform, we may need to use something such as Apache Flink (`https://flink.apache.org/`) or Benthos (`https://www.benthos.dev/`). These tools may not be ones they are familiar with, so they will be required to learn them.

Given that the transformation pipeline is likely to be separate from their services code, we'd probably also want some continuous integration checks that prevent them from making schema changes that break their transforms or the contract since they are tightly coupled to their internal models.

While this approach does have the benefit of providing data through a data contracts-backed interface and solving the transactional guarantees, it has a few drawbacks and limitations. The data generators must now maintain two distinct services that depend on their internal models – the service they are primarily responsible for, and the data transformations. Those transformations may be using tooling they are not familiar with, further adding to their maintenance load and slowing them down.

For those reasons, this isn't a pattern I'd recommend.

Next, we'll look at the transactional outbox pattern, which is a different approach that can be used to achieve a similar outcome, with its own pros and cons.

The transactional outbox pattern

The transactional outbox pattern is a pattern designed primarily to provide transactional guarantees across multiple services and databases. It is commonly used in microservices and other distributed architectures.

With this pattern, you create an *outbox* table in the applications database. Whenever a change is made within the service that we want to publish to our data consumers, we also write the event to the outbox table. A separate process will pick up events from that table and publish them – in our case, to the data contracts-backed interface – so that they can be consumed.

This transactional guarantee is achieved because both the write to the applications table(s) and the outbox table are performed within the same database transaction, as a *single unit of work*. Therefore, if any of those writes fail or the service itself fails part way through the writes, the entire transaction is rolled back to the previous state.

The following diagram shows the transactional outbox pattern in action:

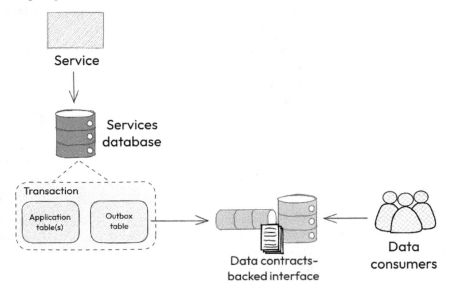

Figure 10.7 – The transactional outbox pattern

The events that are published via the outbox don't need to match the structure of the applications database – and shouldn't. At the time we generate the event, we can use all the context we have available to us to produce an event that matches our data contract and meets the requirements of the downstream consumers. After that, we decouple the structure of our event from the structure of our database, allowing the data generators to make changes to their database with autonomy and without breaking downstream consumption.

Aside from the transactional guarantee, the outbox pattern can also be used to queue events locally before inserting them as a batch into the data warehouse or event streaming platform. Taking that out of the user response flow could improve the performance of the application for its users.

However, the transactional pattern does add some load to the database. We're adding an extra write to our application's critical path. We're also running a separate process that polls or otherwise listens to the events from the outbox table.

Despite those drawbacks, the outbox pattern is a popular solution that provides transactional guarantees across multiple services and data stores.

There's another, similar pattern that we can use to achieve transactional guarantees called the listen-to-yourself pattern. We'll look at that next and see how its benefits and drawbacks compare to the transactional outbox pattern.

The listen-to-yourself pattern

The final pattern we'll introduce is the listen-to-yourself pattern. This is less well-known compared to the transactional outbox pattern but is a good alternative for achieving transactional guarantees across multiple services and databases.

As with the transactional outbox pattern, this provides transactional guarantees by writing to a single data store as a single unit of work and replicating that change later, providing eventual consistency. The difference is that this data store is not the applications database, but a secondary datastore – typically, an event streaming platform or message broker.

Later, a separate process will pick up events from that stream and write them to our applications database. The message broker will also replicate that event to any other subscriber, so in our case, we would have another process to write that same event to the data contracts-backed interface so that they can be consumed.

The following diagram shows the listen-to-yourself pattern:

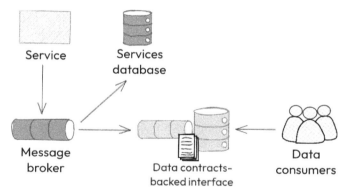

Figure 10.8 – The listen-to-yourself pattern

If our data contracts-backed interface is provided as an event streaming platform, then we can use that rather than a separate message broker, with those events already matching the schema of the data contract.

This pattern does reduce a bit of the load on the database compared to the outbox pattern since we're no longer writing each change to it twice. The performance may also be better for the user, depending on how quickly we can write to the message broker.

The listen-to-yourself pattern is also useful if the database the application is using has limited support for transactions across tables, which prevents us from using the transactional outbox pattern.

However, the applications database itself is now eventually consistent, which means it may take some time before that change is reflected in its database. So, if the user of the service makes a request immediately to get the current state, it may be missing the latest changes, which could be unexpected.

Another consideration is that depending on the message broker we're using, we may receive the events out of order and/or duplicate events. We may need to use a different message broker that guarantees the order, and for duplicates, we would need to ensure that the writes to our services database are idempotent.

Summary

We have concluded this book by looking at what it is like working with data contracts in practice. We started this chapter by looking at how to design a data contract, going step-by-step through identifying the purpose of the contract, considering the trade-offs the data generator needs to make, defining the agreed data contract, and deploying it to production.

Then, we looked at how to monitor and enforce those data contracts, including the definition itself, and then, once it is in production, the quality, performance, and dependability of the data. We discussed how, with data quality, there are two types we need to monitor: those we predicted in advance, and those we didn't. After this, we discussed how we can detect those issues at different places in our architecture.

Finally, we looked at how to publish data to the data contract. We described why you might need to implement transactional guarantees if your data needs a high level of consistency between the source system and the data contract and introduced some publishing patterns to aid with publishing data, along with their benefits and drawbacks.

With these best practices, we have everything we need to drive data quality with data contracts! Congratulations! I hope that with this knowledge about the use of data contracts, you succeed in creating a truly data-driven organization that gets real business value from its data.

Further reading

For more information on the topics that were covered in this chapter, please see the following resources:

- *RFCs for Engineering Organizations*: `https://github.com/jakobo/rfc`
- *Data Mesh Architecture: Designing Data Products*: `https://www.datamesh-architecture.com/data-product-canvas`
- *Is observability just monitoring with another name?*, by Charity Majors: `https://www.honeycomb.io/blog/observability-whats-in-a-name`
- *The Dead Letter Queue pattern*, by Andrew Jones: `https://andrew-jones.com/blog/the-dead-letter-queue-pattern/`
- *Data Consistency in Microservices Architecture*, by Dilfuruz Kizilpinar: `https://dilfuruz.medium.com/data-consistency-in-microservices-architecture-5c67e0f65256`
- *An Engineer's Guide to Data Contracts*, by Chad Sanderson and Adrian Kreuziger: `https://dataproducts.substack.com/p/an-engineers-guide-to-data-contracts`
- *Pattern: transactional outbox*, by Chris Richardson: `https://microservices.io/patterns/data/transactional-outbox.html`
- *Reliable Microservices Data Exchange with the Outbox Pattern*, by Gunnar Morling: `https://debezium.io/blog/2019/02/19/reliable-microservices-data-exchange-with-the-outbox-pattern/`
- *Transactional Events Publishing At Brex*, by Yingying Tang: `https://medium.com/brexeng/transactional-events-publishing-at-brex-66a5984f0726`
- *Listen to Yourself: A Design Pattern for Event-Driven Microservices*, by Oded Shopen: `https://medium.com/@odedia/listen-to-yourself-design-pattern-for-event-driven-microservices-16f97e3ed066`

Index

Packtpub.com

Subscribe to our online digital library for full access to over 7,000 books and videos, as well as industry leading tools to help you plan your personal development and advance your career. For more information, please visit our website.

Why subscribe?

- Spend less time learning and more time coding with practical eBooks and Videos from over 4,000 industry professionals

- Improve your learning with Skill Plans built especially for you

- Get a free eBook or video every month

- Fully searchable for easy access to vital information

- Copy and paste, print, and bookmark content

Did you know that Packt offers eBook versions of every book published, with PDF and ePub files available? You can upgrade to the eBook version at packtpub.com and as a print book customer, you are entitled to a discount on the eBook copy. Get in touch with us at customercare@packtpub.com for more details.

At www.packtpub.com, you can also read a collection of free technical articles, sign up for a range of free newsletters, and receive exclusive discounts and offers on Packt books and eBooks.

Other Books You May Enjoy

If you enjoyed this book, you may be interested in these other books by Packt:

Data Modeling with Snowflake

Serge Gershkovich

ISBN: 9781837634453

- Discover the time-saving features and applications of data modeling

- Explore Snowflake's cloud-native architecture and features

- Understand and apply modeling concepts, techniques, and language using Snowflake objects

- Master modeling concepts such as normalization and slowly changing dimensions

- Get comfortable reading and transforming semi-structured data

- Work directly with pre-built recipes and examples

- Apply modeling frameworks from Star to Data Vault

Data Literacy in Practice

Angelika Klidas, Kevin Hanegan

ISBN: 9781803246758

- Start your data literacy journey with simple and actionable steps
- Apply the four-pillar model for organizations to transform data into insights
- Discover which skills you need to work confidently with data
- Visualize data and create compelling visual data stories
- Measure, improve, and leverage your data to meet organizational goals
- Master the process of drawing insights, ask critical questions and action your insights
- Discover the right steps to take when you analyze insights

Packt is searching for authors like you

If you're interested in becoming an author for Packt, please visit `authors.packtpub.com` and apply today. We have worked with thousands of developers and tech professionals, just like you, to help them share their insight with the global tech community. You can make a general application, apply for a specific hot topic that we are recruiting an author for, or submit your own idea.

Share Your Thoughts

Now you've finished *Driving Data Quality with Data Contracts*, we'd love to hear your thoughts! Scan the QR code below to go straight to the Amazon review page for this book and share your feedback or leave a review on the site that you purchased it from.

`https://packt.link/r/1837635005`

Your review is important to us and the tech community and will help us make sure we're delivering excellent quality content.

Download a free PDF copy of this book

Thanks for purchasing this book!

Do you like to read on the go but are unable to carry your print books everywhere? Is your eBook purchase not compatible with the device of your choice?

Don't worry, now with every Packt book you get a DRM-free PDF version of that book at no cost.

Read anywhere, any place, on any device. Search, copy, and paste code from your favorite technical books directly into your application.

The perks don't stop there, you can get exclusive access to discounts, newsletters, and great free content in your inbox daily

Follow these simple steps to get the benefits:

1. Scan the QR code or visit the link below

https://packt.link/free-ebook/978-1-83763-500-9

2. Submit your proof of purchase
3. That's it! We'll send your free PDF and other benefits to your email directly

www.ingramcontent.com/pod-product-compliance
Lightning Source LLC
Chambersburg PA
CBHW060559060326
40690CB00017B/3765

*9 7 8 1 8 3 7 6 3 5 0 0 9 *